'ECCE HOM

The Love Poems of Horace

Translation and Commentary by Louis Francis

Bulls Brow Press

BBP

First published 1993 by Bulls Brow Press
Ditchling Common West Sussex BN6 8TN

ISBN 1 898646 00 7

Copyright Louis Francis © 1993

The right of Louis Francis to be identified as the author and translator of this work has been asserted by him in accordance with the Copywright Designs and Patents Act 1988.

All rights reserved. No reproduction copy or transmission of this publication or of any parts thereof may be made without specific written permission or in accordance with the provisions of the Copywright Act 1956 (as amended) and any such unauthorised acts will be subject to prosecution and relevant claims for damages.

British Library Cataloguing-in-Publication Data. A catalogue record for this book is available from the British Library.

Printed by The Short Run Print Company, Windsor, Berkshire. SL4 3BZ.

'TO BRENDA'

CONTENTS

Acknowledgements	4
Foreword	5
Preface	7
Suetonius - The Life of Horace	**13**
Vita Horati	14
Analysis & Commentary	20
The Philosophy of Sexual Gratification	**27**
Introduction	28
Satire I, 2	30
Analysis & Commentary	38
Youthful Endeavours	**49**
Introduction	50
Epode 11 - Inachia	53
Epode 14 - Phryne	55
Epode 15 - Neaera	57
Odes I, 5 - Pyrrha	59
Analysis & Commentary	60
Lydia	**69**
Odes I, 8 - Lydia - in her youth	73
Odes I, 13 - Lydia - in her prime	75
Odes I, 25 - Lydia - growing old	77
Odes III, 9 - Lydia - reconciliation	79
Analysis & Commentary	80
Glycera	**87**
Introduction	88
Odes I, 19 - Glycera 1	91
Odes I, 30 - Glycera 2	93
Odes I, 33 - Glycera 3	95
Analysis & Commentary	96

Chloe	101
Introduction	103
Odes I, 23 - Chloe 1	105
Odes III, 26 - Chloe 2	107
Analysis & Commentary	108
Lyce	111
Introduction	112
Odes III, 10 - Lyce I	115
Odes IV, 13 - Lyce II	117
Analysis & Commentary	118
Ligurinus	123
Introduction	125
Odes IV, I - Ligurinus 1	127
Odes IV, 10 - Ligurinus 2	131
Analysis & Commentary	132
Advice to Others	137
Introduction	138
Odes II, 4 - Phyllis	141
Odes II, 5 - Lalage	143
Odes II, 8 - Barine	145
Odes III, 15 - Chloris	147
Analysis & Commentary	148
Friendship	153
Introduction	154
Odes II, 12 - Terentia (Licymnia)	157
Odes IV, 7 - Torquatus	159
Analysis & Commentary	160
Strange Encounters	165
Introduction	166
Epode 8	169
Epode 12	171
Analysis & Commentary	172
Envoi	177
Postscript to the Life of Horace	178

ACKNOWLEDGEMENTS

I would like to record my thanks and appreciation to the many friends and colleagues who have helped me with this book, especially to Malcolm Willcock who read the early chapters and redirected my approach to Horace when I was seriously off course and to Stephen Instone who read the final version and made valuable suggestions that have been gratefully incorporated.

It would be invidious to neglect to mention the overall debt I owe to the members of the Greek and Latin Department of University College London for their assistance and for their teaching. Most of all and quite beyond all repayment is the debt I owe to Tim Cornell and John North of the History Department of University College London for accepting, where others had doubted.

FOREWORD

This book is concerned with the love poems of Horace and written with the assumption that they reflect autobiographical episodes in his life. The poems are given a fresh translation and are made the subject of an individual analysis and commentary.

A new book about Horace joins an immense number already published and it would be an insensitive and, indeed, a foolhardy author who attempted to join that number without paying attention to, and having due respect for, those that had gone before. To attempt to absorb everything that has been published would be equally foolhardy; on the other hand, to try and make a selection or express a preference may be to court literary suicide, so many and varied are the disparate loyalties that have grown up around so great a poet. Nevertheless, reference points need to be established and by way of an opening statement it is only right that such reference points should be revealed at the very beginning. In order to position the translation into a contemporary context it seemed important to have at hand two widely differing translations, apart not only in time but in treatment and general approach. The two chosen are the Loeb translation of the Odes and Epodes by C. E. Bennett published in 1925 and the Penguin tranlation of The Complete Odes and Epodes by W. G. Shepherd published in 1983. The former is a prose treatment and very much reflects the view of Horace of that time, and indeed the previous half century, so that the uncomfortable, explicit passages are either glossed over or excised completely. In fact the author has refused point blank to translate Epodes 8 and 12 at all. The latter translation is a verse treatment, very racy and reflecting the attitudes of the late nineteen-seventies. It abounds with the notorious Anglo-Saxon expletives, where the text of Horace seems to call for them. 'Autre temps, autre mores' no doubt but the words in question do really belong to the spoken, as opposed to the written, word; are all short, sharp and repellent while the English language is rich in far more mellifluous alternatives more suitable to the urbane language of Horace. However, both versions serve the purpose admirably in helping to position a new translation of Horace between extremes. As regards the Satires, once again the Loeb translation by N. R. Fairclough and first published in 1929 and the Penguin revised translation by N. Rudd published in 1979, have been used as extremes examples. As before the Loeb is a prose treatment and the Penguin a verse treatment.

As regards commentaries on Horace the choice is equally wide but that of E. Fraenkel published by Oxford University Press in 1957 seems to be in the nature of a de rigeur, if rather Olympian, choice while the practical approach of K. Quinn published by St Martin's Press in 1980 brings one back to earth again. It has been pointed out that Fraenkel hardly addresses the love poetry of Horace at all and when he does so it is in a cold, emotionless context. Quinn treats the love poems of Horace in a pragmatic fashion which does not really allow the reader to come to terms with the man himself. However both are solid foundations and invaluable map references to anyone attempting to discover the real Horace behind the Odes. It goes without saying that the work of R. G. M. Nisbet and M. Hubbard published by the Oxford University Press as separate books and the Concordance of Horace by L. Cooper are the rock upom which all else is supported.

This book is structured to be approached at four levels, each level designed to allow readers to absorb as much or as little as may suit their interests or requirements. At the first level, it can be read purely as a series of individual poems in the English language which seek to maintain the original metrical structure of Horace as close as the natural cadences of the English language will allow without rendering the meaning too obscure. At the second level, the individual poems may be read and compared against their original Latin text, that accompanies each translation on the facing page, so that structure and meaning may be compared. At the third level, the poems may be read as groups of poems dedicated to a single subject together with an introductory preface to each group that attempts to place the poems in the context of that group. At the fourth level, the poems, in their groups, are made the subject of an analysis and commentary that seeks, by rendering a line by line, prose translation, to reach a deeper understanding of the content of each poem.

PREFACE

The known facts on which to base any work on Horace are very meagre and while a great deal of writing is based on surmise and speculation, it is precisely that and no more. It is the habit of commentators to analyse his work and then synthesise his motives and from that basis to attempt to recreate his persona. However since his works have also been translated many times and their exact meaning has been the continual source of academic argument, the foundation on which such arguments are based are as insubstantial as shifting sands. Horace still retains his mystery.

Much of the problem lies in the perception of Horace himself that succeeding generations of his admirers have held. There have always been 'fashions' in Horace throughout the two thousand years since his death. These fashions have tended to mould Horace and his works into preconceived notions that may well have done a disservice to his memory. There has never been any argument that he was not a perfect poet of the Augustan age; the argument has always been on whether he was also a man of his age. Whether aestheticism in literature also implied aestheticism in living and perfection in poetical construction also meant perfection in moral standards. When it is commented that Horace wrote poems about physical love, a standard reaction is that he did so at second hand and that he sublimated physical ecstasy into spiritual commentary. It is very hard to reconcile the earlier Epodes, particularly 8 and 12 or the Satire I,2., with this theory. Nor can it really be reconciled with some of his last works, particularly Odes IV,1 and IV,13. It surely was as a man, as well as a poet, that he wrote in his youth *'Tument tibi cum inguina, num, si ancilla aut verna est praesto puer, impetus in quem continuo fiat, malis tentigine rumpi? Non ego' (Satire 1, 2. 116/9) or, in his old age, 'Quo fugit Venus, heu, quove color? Decens quo motus? Quid habes illius, illius, quae spirabat amores, quae me surpuerat mihi'* (Ode IV, 13. 17/20). Yet it has always seemed that Horace, having once been placed on a pedestal for his literary genius, could never be taken down again and admitted to have partaken wholeheartedly of the earthy appetites of his own time.

What may have diverted such a perception is the fact that the works of Horace always seem to have been made indivisible from the books in which they were published. For although Horace's output falls naturally into clear areas of subject matter such as Love, Friendship, Duty, Social Commentary and similar, it is seldom, if ever, presented in these groups so that we can judge by other standards than historical sequence. Yet if this is done there is an immediate awareness of a pattern emerging. His love poems become grouped by the same personalities occurring again and again, as though Horace was passing through a specific emotional encounter each time. It then becomes even more difficult to sustain an argument of sublimated love.

Yet no one would doubt Horace on the subjects of treachery, civil war, fighting a battle, defeat, fear of death or abject surrender. He experienced all of these under Brutus and at Philippi; why doubt him on matters of the heart? Suetonius, the historian of the first/second century AD, when he wrote 'The Life of Horatius Flaccus' had no doubts on Horace's attitude to women and love and he was writing of someone no further away than say, for us, the late Victorian poets. In his brief life of Horace, Suetonius states that Horace was born in Venusia on the 8th of December 65 BC, the son of a freedman, and died on the 27th of November 8 BC. In as much as such matters are of importance, it is now, at the time of writing, around two thousand years since his death. It is a sobering reflection on the constancy of mankind's ambitions and achievements, the range of mankind's perplexities and pursuits, that all of what Horace has to say to us in his poetry is as valid today as it was then, at the beginning of the age of Imperial Rome. What Horace has to say about love, despite his sometimes apparent flippancy and diffidence, is itself equally valid.

There is no record that Horace ever married and in the society in which he lived this is surprising since marriage was apparently a normal state amongst the Establishment, one that, if we are to believe commentators such as Suetonius and Cassius Dio, never seems to have been regarded as a brake upon discreet extra marital intrigue. There are indications in his poems that certain women, on occasion, did act as his hostess as, for instance, Neaera in Ode III 14, on the occasion of Augustus's return from overseas but these hostesses seem to have changed with passing time. Maybe the fact of his humble birth, the son of a freedman, prohibited him from marriage within the higher ranks of society, whereas marriage within his own class would have probably inhibited his social mobility within the level that his poetical skills had gained him access. Horace may equally well have been a confirmed bachelor, satisfied to live an aesthetic, if not an abstemious life.

As regards the impact of love in his life, revealed by his poetry, at least nineteen of the Odes and three of the Epodes are clearly concerned with specific instances with named individuals, women or young men. In addition two of the Epodes are of an erotic and invective nature and two more of the Odes are directed, in a more than emotive manner, to friends. It is from all of these poems together that the attitude of Horace towards the physical, moral and mental impact of love can be gauged, and with it, presumably, that of Imperial Rome, for whom, and about whom, he spoke. Suetonius has left us only the bare, factual bones of Horace; an understanding of the emotional values in his poetry is required to put flesh on them.

In his Satire I, 2, Horace pursues an argument against taking extreme positions in life, gives illustrations then neatly turns the argument into the pursuit of love. The sense of what he has to say is that while some men seek solace in a public brothel where they can pay for such services as they require, some men seek the socially unattainable in pursuing other men's wives, transgressing the social mores and thereby placing themselves in social, financial and even physical jeopardy. Why not seek mutual satisfaction with like minded members of the opposite sex, freedmen or freedwomen as the case may be, where no social barriers are broken and no harm is done. Of course, if desire strikes suddenly, there are always house slaves of either sex on hand to obtain instant relief. It is far better than being caught leaving a brothel by a high minded friend or fleeing from a marriage bed in panic when a husband returns unexpectedly. It is very much the view of a young and rather gauche Horace but nevertheless, the roots from which the poet ultimately sprang.

From there, the pattern of love affairs throughout the progression of the Odes and Epodes, after some earlier problems, soon settles down to some semblance of continuity. Epode 11 is an apparent renunciation of love poetry in favour of love itself. Epode 14 describes the disastrous effect his affair with Phrynea, a freedwoman is having on his work; Epode 15 laments the inconstancy of Neaera, while the famous Ode I, 5, in carefully controlled grief, explains to a rival what tribulation and deceit lies ahead for him with a certain Pyrrha. The first woman that Horace appears to have been more than casually involved with is Lydia, who appears in four Odes, I, 8, 13 and 25 and III, 9 . In the first Horace, an observer, describes the effect of Lydia on a friend, in the second Horace himself is involved, jealously resenting any approach by others to his lover, while in the third, Horace, no doubt repaying past hurts, apparently delivers a devastating broadside against a woman now well past her prime. The last poem on Lydia is about reconciliation and is difficult to fit into a time sequence since Horace admits to being, by this time, under the influence of Chloe and has already dismissed Lydia as being too old. Glycera appears in Odes I, 19, 30 and 33 and she might seem the logical successor to Lydia, in terms of the progression of the Odes. In the first Horace is bent on enticing her to look favourably upon him, in the second he invokes Venus to his aid, while in the third he commiserates with a friend that the lady is far too faithless for either of them.

Chloe is the next to be be mentioned in the sequence, appearing in Odes I, 23 and 26. In the first example she is still a maiden whom Horace seeks to seduce but she persists in clinging to her mother, while in the second, Horace, invokes the Gods to punish her. In Odes III, 10 and IV, 13 Horace addresses his passion to Lyce. The first is one of entreaty asking that she not be of the mould of Ulysses' Penelope but yield to her importunate suitor, Horace. In the second, like Lydia before, Horace addresses the older woman, with compassion rather than counterblast, as one past her prime and with memories of their earlier love. Ligurinus is a youth and in addressing his love to him, in Odes IV, 1 and 10, Horace seems openly to defy convention, addressing a specific Roman name and in homosexual terms.

Away from his own involvements, Horace was keen to offer his advice to others on matters of the heart. Odes II, 4, 5, and 8; and III, 15, are all concerned with this theme. Ode II, 4 is concerned with advising on Phyllis and the problems she presents to his friend, Odes II, 5 and 8 are likewise concerned with Lalage and Barine while in III, 15 Horace speaks directly to the lady herself concerned, Chloris, advising her that she is far too old to continue her youthful and dissolute lifestyle. Many of Horace's poems are to friends, all beautiful, sensible and to the point but at least two stand out as reaching far deeper into their relationship. Ode II, 12 is really addressed to Licymnia, a pseudonym for Terentia the wife of Maecenas, and while it is written ostensibly to Maecenas himself there is no doubt that Horace's own sensibilities are aroused. Ode IV, 7 is addressed to his friend Torquatus and is perhaps the most beautiful in the entire canon. The theme is approaching death, made more poignant by the concurrent fact of awakening spring and the changing seasons.

Epodes 8 and 12 are, at first sight, disturbing displays of invective coupled with irrational obscenity and it is difficult to assess their place in the canon. It is easy, on the one hand, to dismiss them as casual, youthful exercises but difficult, on the other hand, to reconcile this with a feeling that there is something far deeper than this locked within the overall content of their words. Both are, without question, addressed to older women in scathing terms for raddled appearance, intemperate lust and wholly unrealistic sexual expectations from the presumably young Horace. In Epode 8 Horace is apparently accused of impotency because of fastidiousness and retorts that the other party, in relation to the act of love, is decrepit beyonds the bounds of decency and that he will require help to continue despite the surroundings of silk cushions and Stoic literature. In Epode 12 the lady herself does the seducing but taunts Horace with impotence, which, although prompted by loathing on his part, she suggests is connected with his failings as a man. The retention of these two Epodes within Horace's output undoubtedly reflect an angry young man phase in the poet's development but the tangible disgust that runs through the poetry itself is so manifest that it is difficult to believe that they were creations of fancy alone.

Within the poetry of Horace there lies the soul of a man who has been in love many times; observing, encountering, experiencing and commenting upon every aspect of its effect. The range of emotion, from bawdy humour to almost incandescent beauty must serve to engage the sensibilities of all who read it even though it is, at the same time, the voice of a skilled craftsman moulding the written word.

Thus the Horace that arises out of such considerations of emotion is an inwardly passionate man exercising self restraint, even diffidence, as an external defence against over commitment and, perhaps, ridicule. He would not, of course, fit the image of the strong, silent lover of romantic fiction but one senses that inside the shell there existed a need for the companionship of a partner in love and the hedonistic pleasures that the gratification of healthy sexual appetites bring. That he was able to record these in such a detached and objective manner and in such magnificent poetry should neither diminish his standing as a poet nor as a man.

SUETONIUS - THE LIFE OF HORACE

VITA HORATI

Q. Horatius Flaccus, Venusinus, patre ut ipse tradit libertino, et exactionem coactore (ut vero creditum est salsamentario, cum illi quidam in altercatione exprobrasset: "Quotiens ego vidi patrem tuum brachio se emungentem!") bello Philippensi excitus a Marco Bruto imperatore, tribunus militum meruit; victisque partibus venia impetrata scriptum quaetorium comparavit. Ac primo Maecenati, mox Augusto insinuatus non mediocrem in amborum amicitia locum tenuit. Maecenas quantopere eum dilexerit satis testatur illo epigrammate:

> "Ni te visceribus meis, Horati,
> Plus iam diligo, tu tuum sodalem
> Hinno me videas strigosiorem";

sed multo magis extremis iudiciis tali ad Augustum elogio: "Horati Flacci ut mei esto memor"!

Augustus epistolarum quoque ei officium optulit, ut hoc ad Maecenatem scripto significat: "Ante ipse sufficiebam scribendis epistulis amicorum nunc occupatissimus et infirmus Horatium nostrum a te cupio abducere. Veniet ergo ab ista parasitica mensa ad hanc regiam, et nos in epistulis scribendis iuvabit." Ac ne recusanti quidem aut suscensuit quicquam aut amicitiam suam ingerere desiit. Exstant epistulae, e quibus argumenti gratia pauca subieci: "Sume tibi aliquid iuris apud me, tamquam si convictor mihi fueris; recte enim et non temere feceris, quoniam id usus mihi tecum esse volui, si per valitudinem tuam fieri possit." Et rursus: "Tui qualem habeam memoriam, poteris ex Septimio quoque nostro audire; nam incidit ut illo coram fieret a me tui mentio. Neque enim si tu superbus amicitiam nostram sprevisti, ideo nos quoque ἀνθυπερηφανοῦμεν" Praeterea saepe eum inter alios iocos "purissimum penem" et "homuncionem lepidissimum" appellat, unaque et altera liberalitate

THE LIFE OF HORACE

The father of Quintus Horatius Flaccus, a freedman and a tax collector of Venusia, as he himself claims (but in truth he was believed to have been a dealer in salt fish for a certain person in a dispute had taunted him " How often I have seen your father wiping his nose with the arm!") In the war at Philippi, having been recruited by Marcus Brutus, the Commander in Chief, he served as a Military Tribune The parties having been vanquished he returned to Rome, and obtained a written pardon from the Quaestor. Gaining the goodwill at first of Maecenas and, by and by, of Augustus he held a not indifferent position in the friendship of both. To what extent he may have been esteemed by Maecenas is attested sufficiently by that epigram:

> "Unless I love you, Horace, more than
> My own flesh and blood, you may see your
> Most intimate companion a barren mule."

But much more so in the final judgement with the following codicil to Augustus: "Be as mindful of Horatius Flaccus as of me!"
Augustus chose him for the position of secretary as he indicates in a letter to Maecenas: " Before this I was in a position to write letters to my friends, now of ill health and being made busy I desire to take away our Horace from you. He will therefore come from that parasitic table to this regimented existence, and will help to write our letters." And at refusal he showed neither anger nor indeed ceased to advance his friendship. By way of proof I have extracted a few examples from surviving letters: "Take it as something right for you to be near me, if as though you may have been one who lives there with me; for you will have accomplished, not by chance, the right thing, for that is the relationship I have wished to be from me with you, if it is possible to be done in your state of health." And again: "What kind of feelings I have of you, you will also be able to hear from Septimius, for it chanced that he made mention of you in my presence. For if you, so proud, have rejected our friendship, for that reason we will not also be haughty in return." Moreover, amongst other jokes, he often called him "an unadulterated penis" and "a most charming little man," and at one and the same time, by one kindness or another, he made him rich.

locupletavit. Scripta quidem eius usque adeo probavit mansuraque perpetuo opinatus est, ut non modo Saeculare carmen componendum iniunxerit sed et Vindelicam victoriam Tiberii Drusique, privignorum suorum, eumque coegerit propter hoc tribus Carminum libris ex longo intervallo quarto addere; post Sermones vero quosdam lectos nullam sui mentionem habitam ita sit questus: "Irasci me tibi scito, quod non in plerisque eius modi scriptis mecum potissimum loquaris; an vereris ne apud posteros infame tibi sit, quod videaris familiaris nobis esse?" Expressitque eclogam ad se, cuius initium est:

> "Cum tot sustineas et tanta negotia solus,
> Res Italas armis tuteris, moribus ornes,
> Legibus emendes: in publica commoda peccem,
> Si longo sermone morer tua tempora, Caesar."

Habitu corporis fuit brevis atque obesus, qualis et a semet ipsum in saturis describitur et ab Augusto hac epistula: "Pertulit ad me Onysius libellum tuum, quem ego ut excusantem, quantuluscumque est, boni consulo. Vereri autem mihi videris ne maiores libelli tui sint, quam ipse es; sed tibi statura deest, corpusculum non deest. Itaque licebit in sextariolo scribas, ut circuitus voluminis tui sit ὀγκωδέστατος sicut est ventriculi tui."

Ad res Venerias intemperantior traditur; nam speculato cubiculo scorta dicitur habuisse disposita, ut quocumque respexisset ibi ei imago coitus referretur. Vixit plurimum in secessu ruris sui Sabini aut Tiburtini, domusque eius ostenditur circa Tiburni luculum. Venerunt in manus meas et elegi sub titulo eius et epistula prosa oratione quasi commendantis se Maecenati sed utraque falsa puto; nam elegi vulgares, epistula etiam obscura, quo vitio minime tenebatur.

Natus est VI Idus Decembris L. Cotta et L. Torquato consulibus. decessit V Kl. Decembris C. Marcio Censorino et C.

Indeed, he very much approved of his writings and what is more he was of the opinion that they would endure for ever, that he enjoined him to compose not only the Secular Hymn but also for the victory over the Vindelicans of his stepsons Tiberius and Drusus, and he next compelled him to add, after a long interval, a fourth to the three books of writings. After a perusal of the Epistles and Satires, moreover, he must have complained that there was no mention of himself therein: "Know anger to be with me, that in the majority of cases in your writings you do not speak with me, rather otherwise. Do you stand in fear lest in the future ill repute might be before you, because you may be seen to be a friend of us?" *And he compelled [from Horace] the reference to himself of which the beginning is:*

"Caesar, so many and so great the tasks you sustain alone,
Italy you protect with arms, provide with morals and with
Laws improve: I may commit a fault against public good if,
With long Epistles, I detain the attention of your time."

In bodily appearance he was short and also stout, and as he once described himself in a satire and Augustus in this letter: "Onysius has brought to me your little book, which I consider good and can excuse, however small it is. However you seem to me to fear lest your books may be greater than you yourself are: but with you it is concerning stature, it is not concerning too little body. Therefore it will be permitted to write on a small pot that the circumference of your roll of manuscript may be more bulky, as is the your stomach."

As regards matters relating to Venus he was given to intemperance; for he is said to have had a bedroom fitted with mirrors and harlots so arranged that whithersoever he might look in that place, images of coitus might be reflected. He lived mostly in retreat in the country on his Sabine or Tiburtine villa, it may be seen near the little grove of Tiburnus.

Elegies and a letter in prose, under his inscription, purporting to be a commendation from Maecenas have come into my hand but I think both counterfeit; For the Elegies are ordinary and the letter likewise obscure which fault he kept to a minimum. He, being born the sixth day of the Ides of December in the consulate of Lucius Cotta and Lucius Torquatus, died on

Asinio Gallo consulibus post nonum et quinquagesimum diem quam Maecenas obierat, aetatis agens septimum et quinquagesimum annum, herede Augusto palam nuncupato, cum urgente vi valitudinis non sufficeret ad obsignandas testamenti tabulas. Humatus et conditus est extremis Esquiliis iuxta Maecenatis tumulum.

the fifth day of the Kalends of December in the consulate of Gaius Marcus Censurinus and Gaius Asinus Gallus, fifty-nine days after Maecenas had died, living to the fifty-seventh year. Naming Augustus heir publicly since the pressing force on his state of health caused him an inability to sign a last will and testament on a tablet, he was made ready for burial and interred at the far end of the Esquiline, near the tomb of Maecenas.

ANALYSIS & COMMENTARY

The opening lines of the Vita, 1 - 6, give us a sparse summary of the early years of Horace, facts on his birth place, his father, that, as a young man, he was caught up in the civil war that followed the assassination of Julius Caesar and served in the post of a military tribune, unfortunately on the losing side and that, according to conventional theory he apparently purchased a post in the civil service. It is possible, as Fraenkel and others have done, to fill in some of the gaps from Horace's own writings but these fall far short of continuity. Certainly he attended school in Rome rather than in Venusia and followed that schooling by attending university at Athens. While there he fell under the sway of Marcus Brutus, whether by conviction or by coercion, and in the second battle of Philippi he discarded his shield and fled with others. He eventually returned to Rome to find his inheritance confiscated and himself penniless. How exactly he found the money to purchase his civil service post is not revealed or even surmised at by Fraenkel and others. Beyond that, nothing; Suetonius takes us swiftly on towards his association with Augustus and Maecenas.

Q. Horatius Flaccus ... patre ... libertino ... exactionem coactore succinctly sets the scene 'the son of a freedman from Venusia who was a collector of auction monies'. By way of gentle debunking, this is followed, in parenthesis, by **ut vero ... salsimentario ... brachio se emungentem!** 'but it has been said his father was a salt fish dealer and wiped his nose on his arm'. This passage says as much about the class perceptions and divisions of Roman society as it does about the poet's origins, one is left with the impression that a **salsimentario** was the bottom of the heap while a **coactore** was not much of an improvement. **Bello Philippensi excitus a Marco Bruto imperatore, tribunus militum meruit** ' He was recruited by Marcus Brutus ... and served as a military tribune' Again this is succinct to the point of obscurity and raises more questions than it answers. From student at university to a military tribune in the field of battle hints either at desperation on the part of Brutus or a cavalier attitude to the exigencies of war. Had Horace any pretences to be a member of the establishment it would be understandable but for the son of a freedman to be thus exalted is puzzling. Again, a military tribune on the losing side in a civil war ought, in the inevitable postscriptions that followed, to have forfeited his life, whether he fled the field or not. Yet, **victisque ... scriptum ... comparavit.** has always been taken as saying that after the defeat he returned to Rome and obtained a post as quaestor's clerk. Is it possible that **victisque partibus venia impetrata scriptum quaestorium comparavit** can have an alternative meaning? Such as 'the parties having been vanquished and forgiveness having been obtained, he was pardoned by the Quaestor's office'. Fraenkel mentions that there is no other evidence that Horace obtained a civil service post since nowhere in his writings does he say so. Such an alternative reading explains much, negates no known fact and would seem to fit the circumstances of the time far more readily.

If so, we have Horace back in Rome in very straitened circumstances and Suetonius goes on with **Ac primo Maecenati, mox Augusto insinuatus ... amicita ... tenuit** 'Having gained the goodwill first of Maecenas, then of Augustus, he held the friendship of both.' Fraenkel comments on the use, by Suetonius, of the verb **insinuo** as being meant as a reprehensible act, presumably with connotations of homosexuality. He suggests that from one writing at the time of Hadrian this would have been a natural assumption and that it should be dismissed from consideration for that reason. Surely there can be no valid reason why such a consideration should not be admitted; it remains a probability that the Rome of that time, under the influence of an inherited Greek ethos, would countenance such behaviour. Certainly Horace himself leaves us in no doubt that he sought solace in homosexual as well as heterosexual liasions, as evidenced in his poetry. However, having admitted the fact as a possibility, it need not receive any undue emphasis.

Maecenas quantopere ... dilexerit ... illo epigrammate 'How much Maecenas esteemed Horace is shown by this epigram' followed by the epigram in question, **Ni te visceribus, Horati ... hinno me videas strigosiorem,** 'Unless I love you more than my own flesh and blood, Horace ... see me as a barren mule'. As epigrams go, this effort of Maecenas is not amongst the best but it can be made a little better by considering **hinno me** in place of a mythical **Ninnio**, as is usual. This allows us to connect **visceribus, hinno** and **strigosiorem** together to underline the epigram. The mule, genetically incapable of siring progeny, is used to point the affection of Maecenas for Horace in comparison with his own flesh and blood, presumably children. It is a revealing insight into the sort of affection implied, that of a father to a son, rather than to a lover and may serve to focus our attention away from the use of the verb **insinuo** used at the beginning of this section. If this reading is accepted it both elevates the status of the epigram and establishes an important point in a relationship. **Sed multo ... extremis iudicis ... Augustum elogio: "Horati Flacci ut mei esto memor"**! further underlines this paternal affection; 'Much more so in the final judgement ... to Augustus: "be as mindful of Horace as of myself"!' The words are surely more those of a father asking an executor to look after a son than someone bequeathing his lover to another man.

The next passage **Augustus epistolarum ... "ante ipse ... abducere"** shows us Augustus, by letter, exercising the prerogative of power by demanding that Maecenas release Horace from his service to serve Augustus as a personal secretary. One must surely ask at this point the question that if Horace was already employed as a clerk in the civil service, why would Augustus ask Maecenas for his services? Surely a mere transfer of employment within the Imperial administration would serve; Maecenas would have no say in the matter at all! Granted that in the early days of the Principate, Augustus was careful not to be seen in the use of dictatorial power, the transfer of a lowly clerk would not be seen as an undue usurpation of power. This is followed by **Veniet ... ad hanc regiam ... scribendis iuvabit**, a passage which, to quote Fraenkel, 'has time and again been made the object of apalling distortions'[p.18]. Certainly it would have raised Republican hackles if it had been given the sort of translation that considers **regiam** in the context of royalty but it is quite clearly written at a time when no sensible Roman would give it that connotation. Rome was then still theorectically more a republic than a monarchy when the thought of a regal dynasty was still an anathema. The term **regiam** could then be seen to have been used in opposition to **parasitica** and the meaning 'regular' or 'regimented' as opposed to 'irregular' or 'casual'. This could then be taken as a reference to the different households and lifestyles of Augustus and Maecenas, the one ordered by some form of protocol, the other by the casual nature of artistic acquaintance. The passage could therefore be considered as 'He will therefore come from that disorderly house to this well ordered existence and will help to write our letters.' This avoids any sinister references to regal power and the rather convoluted argument that Fraenkel submits to accept **regiam** in its regal sense. Even the use of the royal 'our' might well be seen as an emendation on Suetonius's part who, in the second century, could not envisage the Emperor using the first person in personal correspondence.

Thus, **Ac ne ... suscensuit ... amicitiam suam ... desiit** 'at his refusal he showed neither anger nor ceased to advance his friendship', becomes more understandable, the refusal of a request rather than a command. Certainly Augustus's reply, **"Sume tibi ... convictor mihi fueris ... si per valitudinen ...possit"** 'Take it as right for you to be near me, for that is all I intended, inasmuch as it is possible in your state of health', amplifies this while writing, tongue in cheek, of Horace's transparent excuse of ill health. Augustus's **"Tui qualem ... ex Septimio ... nostro audire ... a me tui mentio. ... si tu superbus ... ideo nos quoque ἀνθυπερηφανοῦμεν'** 'What kind of feelings I retain for you, learn from Septimius, ... that I shall not be haughty in return.', shows no ill feeling but one is struck, however, by the heavy humour of Augustus and the rather cumbersome Latin employed. If this was his normal written style, Augustus certainly did need the services of someone like Horace to act as amanuensis! As to the use of the Greek compound, ανθυπερηφανουμεν, Fraenkel is of the opinion that Augustus, like all educated Romans, used Greek loan words as a matter of course. The reason that this particular compound is not attested anywhere else, he suggests, is that Augustus 'coined it on the spur of the moment'. Such a facility, on the part of Augustus, is not the only interpretation of its use; a Greek slave, acting as amanuensis and taking dictation, might equally well have coined it in default of an exact Latin equivalent. The fact of a Greek slave being able to make use of double compound verbs need not surprise us. Those serving the higher levels of Roman society in a secretarial capacity would undoubtably have been well educated, a fact that might also explain the sometimes cumbersome Latin. **Praeterea ... inter alios jocos ... "purissimum penem" et "homuncionem lepidissimum" appellat ... locupletavit,** 'Among other jokes he called him "unadulterated penis" and "effeminate little man" but by kindness, made him rich.' It would seem implicit that Augustus would use such terms in speech only and then only in the company of men. Nor should any undue emphasis be placed on their having any homosexual connotation. Such jocularity amongst men is, and presumably has always been, commonplace. Horace would only need to be less adventurous in sexual encounters than was the norm to be the butt of such humour. Used as such they are indeed terms of affection and would be accepted as such.

Scripta quidem ... privignorum suorum, 'He thought so much of his writings that he commissioned the Secular Hymn and the victory of his stepsons, Tiberius and Drusus, over the Vindelicans', gives us an insight into Horace's middle years and output and, presumably, his blossoming in Roman society. **Eumque coegerit ... Carminum libris ... quartum addere** 'he compelled him, after a long interval, to add a fourth book of Odes.' and, **post Sermones ... lectos nullam sui mentionem ... questus "Irasci ... scito ... videaris familiaris nobis esse?" ... Expressitique eclogam ad se ...** 'After perusal of the Epistles and Satires he complained that there was no mention of himself, "are you afraid to be seen to be a friend of mine?" and he forced Horace to write an Epistle, [2, 1]. This passage that gives us an insight into the burst of activity in Horace's later years culminating in Ode IV, 15. This Ode, fullsome in its praise of Augustus, is almost too good to be true. When viewed dispassionately it can be seen as being as much intrinsic sarcasm as noble sentiment. Was Horace reacting to pressure by seeming to yield but secretly sending up Augustus.

The passage beginning **Habitu corporis,** to ὀγκωδέστατος **sicut est ventriculi tui",** saying, in effect,'in bodily appearance he was short and stout and Augustus complained that his latest offering is as small as himself, so much so that it could have been written on a small pot.' is often dismissed as heavy humour on Augustus's part. Fraenkel is of the opinion that the reference to the small pot was to the habit of using broken pottery surfaces for writing purposes in default of papyrus. This, as a joking reference, seems almost too laboured, even for Augustus. It is equally likely that Augustus was referring not to the physical size of the manuscript but the actual contents. Not in fact to the length of the work but to what it has to say, presumably about himself; that, in effect, there was insufficient mention of himself in a favourable light. **... sed tibi statura deest,**

corpusculum non deest, can be interpreted as meaning 'but with you the length of the work is not important but the substance of the work is'. The reference to the small pot is therefore not about circumference but about capacity. It is idle to speculate but such sentiments could well have been occasioned by the same Ode IV, 15, mentioned above, with the corollary that Augustus could well have been aware of its true nature.

Ad res Venerias ... referretur is a passage delicately ignored by most commentators and Fraenkel dismisses it, rather, as 'filthy detail'. It succinctly states that it was maintained that Horace was in the habit of having mirrors in his bedroom so that he could see himself making love from all angles. Well, it would seem a natural enough indulgence if one has power, money and the inclination; it would be a saintly man indeed who has not entertained such fantasies himself. The only disturbing note is the use, in the plural sense, of **scorta**, 'prostitutes'. One is left with the vision of group sex, since it would be physically impossible for one man. There is a nagging remembrance of the later exploits of Tiberius, also related by Suetonius, and it would have the effect of turning an innocent fantasy into a voyeuristic interlude. In both cases Suetonius admits it as hearsay but while posterity has always credited Tiberius with such actions, it has tried to ignore similar actions attributed to Horace.

Vixit plurimum ... Tiburni luculum, 'he lived mostly in his villa at Tiburnum near the little grove of Tiburnus' merely echoes what Horace has to say in his poetry. **Venerunt in manus ... elegi sub titulo eius ... quo vitio minime tenebatur** 'I have to hand a number of works with his inscription but obviously counterfeit, not being of the quality of his work', is a passage, as Fraenkel comments, that has quite clearly been shorn of most of its substance. To make any sort of biographical sense it must have been preceded by a list of his acknowledged works. **Natus est ..., decessit ... herede Augustus ... Humatus et conditus ... juxta Maecenatis tumulum**, 'he was born on eighth of December 65 BC, dying suddenly on twenty-seventh of November 8 BC, leaving Augustus his heir. He was buried near the tomb of Maecenas' completes the life.

THE PHILOSOPHY OF SEXUAL GRATIFICATION.

THE PHILOSOPHY OF SEXUAL GRATIFICATION

INTRODUCTION

Fraenkel considers Satire I, 2, to be probably the earliest of the Satires. Whether or not this is so, its theme, on the folly of going to extremes in all things, is carefully steered toward the gratification of sexual desire. In its entire length, the theme of love or the emotion of love is scarcely mentioned, merely the physical satiation of the restlessness it engenders and the means and ends to which men will go to achieve this. Horace begins by contrasting two attitudes to wealth, using the classical μέν and δέ formula, of a certain Tigellius and Fufidius. However within each section is also concealed another set of μέν and δέ clauses.

Tigellius, a poet, a singer and, apparently, the inheritor of wealth which he squanders on loose living and with the low life of the City; prodigal in his gifts to them but, on the other hand, never sparing any to friends in dire need. At his death there are, understandably, mixed emotions.

Contrasting this, Fufidius, a moneylender, hoards his wealth to himself, lending out capital at exhorbitant interest rates and pursuing erring debtors to their ruin. Yet, on the other hand, he gets no enjoyment from his wealth, does not spend money on himself and lives the life of a recluse, lonely and unloved.

Horace thus makes a point about extreme positions in life and goes on to illustrate further. Maltinus goes about the City in clothing that falls right to the ground, revealing nothing: a man of fashion lifts the hem of his garment so high that his genitals are revealed. Rufillus smells of perfume: Gargonius does not care to conceal his body odour. Similarly, some men yearn after women who cover themselves respectably from head to foot, in other words Roman matrons; other men are content to seek women in brothels where all is revealed before any commitment is made. Yet the punishments and retributions for adultery are many and varied; suicide, whipping to death, flight and subsequent ambush by bandits, financial ruin, being raped by stable boys at the wronged husband's command or painful emasculation by a similarly wronged husband. The social stigma that is associated with frequenting brothels can be equally oppressive.

Horace then cautions against courtesans, who falling between matrons and the women of the brothel, nevertheless are to be likewise avoided. In the end they cost men dear, they have been known to squander their inheritances on such women while boasting that they have avoided the trap of adultery. To what end? asks Horace; you have lost wealth, position and good name in the process. Quoting the case of Villius, the lover of Sulla's daughter Fausta, Horace draws the example of a man brought to ruin by confusing what is desired with what is to be avoided. It is like buying a horse, cover up the obvious good points, consider what is left and make your decision accordingly. What you pursue, be prepared to eat! Observe nature and act accordingly, recognise hunger and thirst for what they are, basic appetites to be quenched by basic means. If you pursue married women be prepared for the obstacles; her gown, her litter, her attendants, her hairdresser, her guards and her husband, returning unexpectedly. Be prepared for her wiles, excuses and desires; 'another time', 'when my husband is away', 'have you finished already, I want more!' Make love in peace and not with the fear that a thunderous knocking at the door will portend a vengeful husband with the inevitable consequences. Consternation, recrimination, accusation, abject fear and ignominious flight, clothes in hand in the expectation of losing one's life as well as one's dignity. Misery lies in being caught out; far better a willing and unattached partner with no social standing.

If there is no one better at hand than house slaves when desire strikes, then take what is offered. For when you achieve desire, your partner, woman or boy, can be what you wish, you call them by what name you will and experience what you wish.

SATIRE I, 2

Ambubaiarum collegia, pharmacopolae,
mendici, mimae, balatrones, hoc genus omne
maestum ac sollicitum est cantoris morte Tigelli:
quippe benignus erat. contra hic, ne prodigus esse
dicatur metuens, inopi dare nolit amico,
frigus quo duramque famem propellere possit.
hunc si percontaris, avi cur atque parentis
praeclaram ingrata stringat malus ingluvie rem,
omnia conductis coemens obsonia nummis:
sordidus atque animi quod parvi nolit haberi,
respondet. laudatur ab his, culpatur ab illis.
Fufidius vappae famam timet ac nebulonis,
dives agris, dives positis in faenore nummis:
quinas hic capiti mercedes exsecat, atque
quanto perditior quisque est, tanto acrius urget;
nomina sectatur modo sumpta veste virili
sub patribus duris tironum. "maxime" quis non
"Iuppiter!" exclamat, simul atque audivit? "at in se
pro quaestu sumptum facit hic." vix credere possis
quam sibi non sit amicus, ita ut pater ille, Terenti
fabula quem miserum gnato vixisse fugato
inducit, non se peius cruciaverit atque hic.
　　Si quis nunc quaerat "quo res haec pertinet?" illuc:
dum vitant stulti vitia, in contraria currunt.
Maltinus tunicis demissis ambulat; est qui
inguen ad obscenum subductis usque facetus.
pastillos Rufillus olet, Gargonius hircum.
nil medium est. sunt qui nolint tetigisse nisi illas
quarum subsuta talos tegat instita veste:
contra alius nullam nisi olenti in fornice stantem.
quidam notus homo cum exiret fornice "macte
virtute esto" inquit sententia dia Catonis:
"nam simul ac venas inflavit taetra libido,
huc iuvenes aequum est descendere, non alienas

THE PHILOSOPHY OF SEXUAL GRATIFICATION

*The circle of flute players, purveyors of quack medicines,
beggars, transvestites, jesters, and all that type of person
was cast down and disturbed at the death of the poet Tigellius:
to be sure he was prodigal. Against this, being afraid he might be
considered too prodigal, he would be unwilling to give to a friend,
what could be able to drive forth malnutrition and harsh cold.
If you may have enquired why he wickedly strips off the illustrious
possessions of grandfather, and also parents, with gluttony
collecting all the money together and buying foods to eat with bread:
he answers, because he does not wish to be thought paltry and of
petty inclination. He is commended by some, condemned by others.
Fufidius, the worthless wretch, rich in lands, rich in money from
interest bearing capital and good for nothing, fears public opinion.
This fellow takes away five times the interest from the capital
And also how little each is from ruin so much harder he presses;
He pursues the collateral of young men, with stern fathers, having
only just put on the toga of manhood. Who would not exclaim "Great
Jupiter!" and at the same time that he has heard it? But from the
profit does he take a proportion for himself? You scarcely believe
how he is no friend to himself, like that father, introduced in the
story by Terence, who by banishing the son, to have lived in abject
misery, never crucified himself more cruelly than this one.*

 *If anyone should now ask "how is this matter pertinent?" thither:
As they seek to escape a fault fools hasten towards its opposite
Maltinus promenades with tunic lowered to the ground; it is fashionable
to pull the hem of it up to the private parts which is disgusting.
Rufillus emits a smell of aromatic lozenges, Gargonius of armpits.
It is not a middle course. Those who would be unwilling to touch unless covered in
garments of such a kind which are fringed at the bottom:
Against this another, nobody unless standing in an odorous brothel.
A certain acquaintance to a man coming out of a brothel, "hail to thee,
be with strength" he said in the well-established sentiments of Cato,
"for at the same time uncontainable lust inflames young men's veins
it is better to come down here, to such a place, not to grind through*

*permolere uxores." "Nolim laudarier," inquit
"sic me," mirator cunni Cupiennius albi.*

    *Audire est operae pretium, procedere recte
qui moechis non voltis, ut omni parte laborent,
utque illis multo corrupta dolore voluptas
atque haec rara cadat dura inter saepe pericla.
hic se praecipitem tecto dedit; ille flagellis
ad mortem caesus; fugiens hic decidit acrem
praedonum in turbam, dedit hic pro corpore nummos,
hunc perminxerunt calones; quin etiam illud
accidit ut quidam testis caudamque salacem
demeteret ferro. "iure" omnes: Galba negabat.*

    *Tutior at quanto merx est in classe secunda,
libertinarum dico, Sallustius in quas
non minus insanit quam qui moechatur. at hic si,
qua res, qua ratio suaderet, quaque modeste
munifico esse licet, vellet bonus atque benignus
esse, daret quantum satis esset, nec sibi damno
dedecorique foret. verum hoc se amplectitur uno,
hoc amat et laudat: "matronam nullam ego tango."
ut quondam Marsaeus, amator Originis ille,
qui patrium mimae donat fundumque laremque,
"nil fuerit mi" inquit "cum uxoribus umquam alienis."
verum est cum mimis, est cum meretricibus, unde
fama malum gravius quam res trahit. an tibi abunde
personam satis est, non illud quicquid ubique
officit evitare? bonam deperdere famam
rem patris oblimare, malum est ubicumque. quid inter-
est in matrona, ancilla peccesne togata?*

    *Villius in Fausta Syllae gener, hoc miser uno
nomine deceptus, poenas dedit usque superque
quam satis est, pugnis caesus ferroque petitus,
exclusus fore, cum Longarenus foret intus.
huic si mutonis verbis mala tanta videnti
diceret haec animus: "quid vis tibi? numquid ego a te*

other men's wives." " I am unwilling to be praised" said
Cupiennius, admirer of pudenda in white, "for such a quality."

It is worth attention to hear, you who wish retribution to
advance on adulterers, that on all sides they may be punished,
and that for them the enjoyment is corrupted by much agony
and such rare enjoyment may fall often between cruel punishments.
This one gave up, throwing himself from a roof; that one cut to
death with whips; this one fleeing away fell in with a gang of
violent predators; this one surrendered wealth to save body,
another was buggered by stable boys; but also indeed that it
has happened that the salacious penis and testicles have been
hacked off with cold steel. "Justly so" from all: Galba denies.

But how much safer it is with second class merchandise,
with freedwomen I say, Sallustius who is more than a little
mad on the subject, more so than any adulterer. but if he
wished to be good and generous, by any means and by whatever
reckoning, he might be persuaded, by whatsover liberal moderation
to give an amount, not enough as might be about to bring ruin and
disgrace upon himself. In actual fact, he at once embraces,
loves and sanctifies himself: "I, myself, touch no matrons
as that Marsaeus, a founder of the race and such a lover, who gave his
inheritance, estate and household gods to an actress "it will
never be for me" he said, " ever with other men's wives."
But the harm to public esteem it attracts is heavier with
actresses than it is with prostitutes. Or, to hinder the
extravagant role, is it not enough for you to avoid it wherever
and whatever the circumstances? To lose good public esteem, to
squander a patronage is terrible at any time. What concern is
it, whether you sin with a matron or with a slave girl in a toga?

Villius, by Fausta, once son-in-law to Sulla, miserable wretch,
deceived by the lady's name, suffered continuous punishment, enough
and more than enough, having been beaten by the fist, assailed by steel
and shut out in the forum while Longarenus penetrated within.
If this one, facing so much evil, might deliver silent words to
the soul of the inner man: "what would you? Did I, from you, ever

magno prognatum deposco consule cunnum
velatumque stola, mea cum conferbuit ira?"
quid responderet? "magno patre nata puella est."
at quanto meliora monet pugnantiaque istis
dives opis natura suae, tu si modo recte
dispensare velis ac non fugienda petendis
immiscere. Tuo vitio rerumne labores,
nil referre putas? Quare, ne paeniteat te,
desine matronas sectarier, unde laboris
plus haurire mali est quam ex re decerpere fructus.
nec magis huic inter niveos viridisque lapillos
(sit licet hoc, Cerinthe, tuum) tenerum est femur aut crus
rectius, atque etiam melius persaepe togata est.
adde huc quod mercem sine fucis gestat, aperte
quod venale habet ostendit, nec, si quid honesti est,
iactat habetque palam, quaerit quo turpia celet.
regibus hic mos est, ubi equos mercantur: opertos
inspiciunt, ne, si facies, ut saepe, decora
molli fulta pede est, emptorem inducat hiantem,
quod pulchrae clunes, breve quod caput, ardua cervix.
hoc illi recte: ne corporis optima Lyncei
contemplere oculis, Hypsaea caecior illa
quae mala sunt spectes. "O crus, O bracchia!" verum
depugis, nasuta, brevi latere ac pede longo est.
matronae praeter faciem nil cernere possis,
cetera, ni Catia est, demissa veste tegentis.
si interdicta petes, vallo circumdata (nam te
hoc facit insanum), multae tibi tum officient res,
custodes, lectica, cicniflones, parasitae,
ad talos stola demissa et circumdata palla,
plurima quae invideant pure apparere tibi rem.
Altera, nil obstat; Cois tibi paene videre est
ut nudam, ne crure malo, ne sit pede turpi;
metiri possis oculo latus. An tibi mavis
insidias fieri pretiumque avellier ante
quam mercem ostendi? "leporem venator ut alta

demand from the Consul, when my passion began to boil,
a high;y born prostitute who had been clothed in a stola?"
What might he reply? "The girl is a noble father's daughter."
But how much better nature herself advises fighting these
costly desires, if only you may wish to arrange correctly
and not mix together what to flee from with what ought
to be sought. Do you think the things you suffer from not
your problem to solve? Cease to pursue matrons, thereby
you need not repent whence the effort to reach down more
evil is to take away what enjoyment there is from the thing.
No more straighter thigh or leg has been visible between
precious emeralds or pearls (this may not be so of yours,
Cerinthus), and also that the prostitute is very often better.
Also what merchandise she carries is uncovered, without pretence.
What she has for sale she exposes to view, if she is lovely,
she displays what she has openly, she does conceal the unsightly.
This is the caprice of princes, when they buy horses: they examine
them covered, it directs the buyer to the mouth so that when the
external form is beautiful with fabulous haunches, small head and
stately neck it is not being propped up with tender hooves.
This is the right way. Not to consider the best of the body
with the eyes of Lynx while you carefully consider the faults
with the blindness of Hypsaea. "O legs, O arms!" True but she
is thin buttocked with a large nose, short flanks and a long foot.
As regards matrons, you cannot distinguish more than the face,
unless she is Catia; a garment, worn to the floor, covers the rest.
If you will seek forbidden fruit surrounded by a rampart (for this
is what is making you insane), then many things will impede you,
Guardians, a litter, heaters of curling irons, social parasites,
the stola worn down to the ankles and surrounded by an outer robe,
countless obstacles which prevent things becoming visible to you.
With the other, no problem: when in Coan silk, she is almost naked
for you to see, no ill-shaped legs, she may not have unsightly feet;
you can measure the figure with the eye. Or, before the merchandise
is shown to you and before you take possession, would you prefer to
become parted from the money? "A huntsman, that in deep snow pursues

in nive sectetur, positum sic tangere nolit,"
cantata et apponit "meus est amor huic similis; nam
transvolat in medio posita et fugientia captat."
Hiscine versiculis speras tibi possit dolores
atque aestus curasque gravis e pectore pelli?
    Nonne, cupidinibus statuat natura modum quem,
quid latura sibi, quid sit dolitura negatum,
quaerere plus prodest et inane abscidere soldo?
num, tibi cum fauces urit sitis, aurea quaeris
pocula? Num esuriens fastidis omnia praeter
pavonem rhombumque? Tument tibi cum inguina, num, si
ancilla aut verna est praesto puer, impetus in quem
continuo fiat, malis tentigine rumpi?
non ego: namque parabilem amo Venerem facilemque.
illam "post paulo," "sed pluris," "si exierit vir."
Gallis, hanc Philodemus ait sibi, quae neque magno
stet pretio neque cunctetur cum est iussa venire.
candida rectaque sit; munda hactenus, ut neque longa
nec magis alba velit quam dat natura videri.
haec ubi supposuit dextro corpus mihi laevum,
Ilia et Egeria est; do nomen quodlibet illi
nec vereor ne, dum futuo, vir rure recurrat,
ianua frangatur, latret canis, undique magno
pulsa domus strepitu resonet, vepallida lecto
desiliat mulier, miseram se conscia clamet,
cruribus haec metuat, doti deprensa, egomet mi.
discincta tunica fugiendum est et pede nudo,
ne nummi pereant aut puga aut denique fama.
deprendi miserum est: Fabio vel iudice vincam.

the hare, may be unwilling to touch one that lies to hand,"
he sings and adds "this is similar to my love; for
she ignores what is already laid out and seeks the fugitive."
You hope with these present little verses to be able to drive
out anguish, passion and also care's burden out of the breast?
   Is it not better to ask what standard nature establishes for
desire, what she is able to bear herself, what, denied, she may
be about to suffer; to seek further and divide solid from void?
Or, when thirst dries up the mouth for you, you ask for a goblet
of gold? Or, being very hungry, you disdain everything except
peacock and turbot. Or, when the genitals are swelling for you, if
a maidservant or boy house slave is at hand, and the impulse may be
gratified immediately, would you prefer to burst with lust?
Not I: for the pleasure I love is easily procured and easily done.
"After a while," But more," "If my husband has gone away," she is
for the Galli, that Philodemus himself asserted, she must not
cost much money nor hesitate when she is commanded to come.
She must be fair and straight up to a point, but no taller nor
more white than what nature may wish and which it gives to be seen.
She is an Ilia or an Egeria when she places, for me, the left side
under the right side, I give to this one whatever name you please.
While I sow my seed, I fear not lest the husband returns from the farm,
the front door battered, the dog bark, the house reverberate all over
with the noise of knocking, the woman, pale, leaps down from the marriage
bed, her miserable maidservant cries aloud for her legs, herself,
having been caught out, afraid for the dowry, I, myself, for me.
It is to be made to flee with dishevelled tunic and barefoot
lest money, public esteem or the fleshy parts of my body suffer harm.
To be caught out is wretched: or with Fabius as judge, I may be the victor.

ANALYSIS & COMMENTARY

One must express disagreement with Fraenkel in regard to many of his points about this Satire; about the content and the structure for instance, and particularly about the important opening role that lines 1 to 22 play.

It seems a reasonable supposition, from an observation of both structure and content, that Horace intended the first twenty-two lines of this Satire to form two identically structured and opposing arguments of eleven lines each, exquisitely balanced and set in the classical μέν *and* δέ mode. In effect, 'On the one hand Tigellius ...', is contrasted with 'on the other hand Fufidius ...'. Therefore, the pivotal phrase **contra hic**, in the first argument does not have the function of jettisoning Tigellius by introducing a new character, as is generally suggested by commentators including Fraenkel; it changes gear, as it were, and introduces another facet of Tigellius's own character, one that gives us some idea of the circumstances of his early demise. It serves to connect, and contrast, **quippe benignus erat** with **ne prodigus esse dicatur metuens,** thus. 'To be sure he was generous. Against this, being afraid he might be said to be too prodigal, ...'. This allows us to see that although Tigellius was prepared to spend his money on his low life companions and did not care what people said, he was not prepared to support a friend in dire poverty with the very staple of existence, **inopi dare nolit amico, frigus quo duramque famem propellere possit.** Which makes into doubly effective satire, **hunc si percontaris ... cur ... stringat ... ingluvie rem, ... coemens obsonia nummis: ... sordidus ... nolit haberi respondet;** in effect, ' If you ask him why he squanders his inheritance buying food that is eaten with bread, he replies so as not to appear mean and paltry'. **Laudatur ab his, culpatur illis** completes the irony. ' He is commended by some, condemned by others.' What we have, therefore, in these opening eleven lines, resembles Hogarth's Rake's Progress in miniature. Tigellius inherits wealth and spends it on riotous living, ignoring a needy friend as well as good counsellors. Bearing in mind the early date of this work we should be prepared to consider that the needy friend in question could have been Horace himself, during those early, penniless days in Rome. It would explain Horace's subsequent coolness towards Tigellius in terms other than professional jealousy. Tigellius is therefore surrounded by people out for a good time, who fawn on him and rapidly help to spend all the money. When he finally dies of excess they mourn the passing of a source of wealth rather than a friend. Returning to the catalogue of occupations that open this Satire, **Ambubaiarum collegia, pharmacopolae, mendici, mimae, balatrones, hoc genus omne**, which could be regarded as a list of professions such as, Flute Players, Pharmacists, Mendicants, Actresses and Clowns, in another context and in the light of what follows, one could be forgiven for taking another view. Tigellius, lately deceased, seems to have suffered the sort of fate that overtook the Hogarthian Tom Rakewell and the people he appears to have mixed with would have likewise undoubtedly helped him on the road to ruin and an early demise. Yet, however odd the assortment of trades, one does not naturally associate them with such activity and the question is prompted whether Horace was using the names as euphemisms. Thus **Ambubaiarum, ... pharmacopolae, mendici, mimae balatrones,** might, in such a context, have hidden meanings. **Ambubaiarum** 'Flute Players' used, euphemistically, to describe exponents of fellatio, **pharmacopolae** to mean 'pushers' - of drugs, poisons and aphrodisiacs, **mendici** to mean 'confidence tricksters', **mimae** to mean 'transvestites' and **balatrones** to mean 'sycophants', **Collegia ... hoc genus omne,** 'The circle of ... and all that type of person', then collectively describes a parasitical growth which exists on the fringe of society and scavenges off it, rather than a group of people that serve it. Alas, considering the transitory and fashionable nature of euphemisms, even in our own day, it is impossible to attach any weight to such a theory.

Fraenkel is rather dismissive of this opening clause, accepting the generally held opinion that it is not all of one theme or about one particular person. Far from it. It is a brilliant opening on the theme of excess, of proceeding without sense of ultimate direction and of seeking the short-term gratification of uncertain appetites and easy solutions to problems not properly thought out.

Tigellius serves as one extreme example; in the next eleven lines, Fufidius as the opposite extreme. Horace sums up Fufidius in a magnificent and devastating couplet, **Fufidius vappae famam timet ac nebulonis, dives agris, dives positis in faenore nummis.** 'Fufidius, the worthless wretch, rich in lands, rich from interest-bearing capital and good for nothing, fears public opinion', must be one of the most damning introduction of any character in literature. At once we are poles apart from the nature of Tigellius; here is a man, conscious of his position in society, who uses money and does not waste it but is apparently just as little use to that society. Once again Horace opens his example on a downbeat, negative note in order to bring out and highlight further details of the character.

Quinas hic capiti mercedes exsecat, 'This one extracts five times the interest from capital' echoes the pivotal phrases of the first section and contrasts facets of the two men. **Atque quanto perditior quisque est, tanto acrius urget** 'and also the nearer his creditors are to ruin, the harder he presses' is the equivalent corollary. **Nomina sectatur ... veste virili ... sub patribus duris ...**, 'he pursues the collateral of young men new to manhood and with stern fathers' expands on Fufidius's methods while **"maxime ... Iuppiter" exclamat ...** 'Who would not exclaim "Great Jupiter" when he hears this', the reaction of society in general. **"At in se pro quaestu sumptum facit hic?"**, "but surely he spends a like proportion on himself?", introduces the paradox of Fufidius to contrast with the paradox of Tigellius. **Vix credere ... non sit amicus** 'You would scarcely believe how little a friend he is to himself.' **Ita ut pater, ille Terenti ... non se peius cruciaverit atque hic** 'like that father, the one in Terence who, by banishing his son lived in misery, never crucified himself as much as this one', completes the paradox. Fufidius hoards his money, gaining no pleasure from it and, like Tigellius, will come to a miserable end.

So, in this way, Horace prepares us for the main point of the Satire. The pursuit of love, or rather, its gratification is similar to the pursuit of money. One should enjoy it without strain, neither placing too much emphasis on the pleasure it brings nor dismissing its capacity to give pleasure in the first instance. Love is an art, not a commodity; creative rather than manipulative.

Lines twenty-three to thirty-six are therefore to be seen as a preamble to this main aim and serve to link the parables of Tigellius and Fufidius in their attitude to money with the attitude of society in general to extreme behaviour. First Horace poses the question, **Si quis nunc quaerat "quo res** haec pertinet?" 'If anyone should now ask "how is this pertinent?", then answers **illuc: dum vitant stulti vitia, in contraria currunt** 'thus: as they seek to escape a fault, fools run to its opposite.' Then examples are given. **Maltinus tunicis demissis ambulat; est qui inguen ad obscenum subductis usque facetus.** in effect, 'Maltinus goes decently covered but it is considered fashionable to pull up the hem and expose the genitals.' Or, **Pastillos Rufillus olet, Gargonius hircum** 'Rufillius smells of scented cachous, Gargonius of armpits.' Horace comments, **nil medium est** 'it is never a compromise.' and steers the argument to the pursuit of love. **Sunt qui nolint tetigisse ... tegat instita veste.** In essence, 'there are those who pursue only married women' is contrasted with, **contra alius nullam nisi olenti in fornice stantem.**, in summary, 'against another unable to perform unless in a foul brothel', Horace closes this preamble with another parable. **Quidam notus homo cum exiret fornice, "macte virtute esto" inquit sententia dia Catonis: "nam simul ac venas inflavit taetra libido, huc iuvenes aequam est descendere, non alienas permolere uxores."** , 'A certain aquaintance said to a man coming out of a brothel, echoing the sentiments of Cato, "Hail to you, be with strength. When lust inflames young men's veins, it is better to come down here, not to grind through other men's wives."' With a final twist, Horace turns the parable around. **"Nolim laudarier" inquit "sic me," mirator cunni Cupennius albi'** "I am unwilling to be praised for such a virtue" said Cupennius, an admirer of pudenda concealed by matronly white robes.' We are left with the question as to whether Cupennius was the user of the brothel or so well known as a an adulterer as to be the censure of all in Rome. However, since Horace, in lines thirty-seven to forty-six, begins to develop his main theme with a catalogue of the terrible punishments visited on such adulterers, we can assume the latter case.

Audire est operae pretium, ... qui moechis non voltis, ... utque illis multo corrupta dolore voluptas ... inter saepe pericla, saying in effect, 'For everyone who wishes retribution to fall on adulterers, it is worth paying attention as to just how there are punished and that their brief pleasure is accompanied by much pain.' Horace then lists their misfortunes. **Hic se praecipitem tecto dedit** 'this one consigned himself to jumping off a roof.' **Ille flagellis ad mortem caesus** 'that one cut to death with whips.' **Fugiens**

hic decidit acrem praedonum in turbam 'this one, fleeing, fell in with a gang of cutthroats.' **Dedit hic pro corpore nummos** 'this one surrendered money for his life.' **Hunc perminxerunt calones** 'another was buggered by stable boys.' Finally, having titillated his readers, Horace gives them what they have been waiting for, **quin etiam illud accidit, ut quidam testis caudamque salacem demeteret ferro'**... it has happened that the salacious penis and testicles concerned have been hacked off with cold steel.' Horace sums up popular feeling, **"Iure" omnes** '"Justly so" from all. Then a wry twist, **Galba negabat** 'Galba disagreeing'; Galba, being both a *juris consultus*, and, apparently, a well known adulterer.

Lines forty-seven to sixty-three explore the theory that love affairs with freedwomen are much safer and equally satisfying, unless, that is, one takes it to extremes! **Tutior at quanto merx est in classe secunda, libertinarum dico,** thus Horace would seem to be quoting Sallust, 'But how much safer it is with second-class merchandise, with freedwomen I say.' But then qualifies it by explaining, **Sallustius in quas non minus insanit quam qui moechatur**, 'but then, Sallust is more than a little mad upon the subject, more so than any adulterer.' Horace then returns to Cato's theme, on the use of brothels, **at hic si, qua res, qua ratio ... quaque modeste ... vellet ... daret quantum satis esset, nec sibi damno ... foret**, saying, in fact, 'but if he (Sallust) wished he could easily afford to patronise a paying establishment and not risk shame and ruin by unwise affairs.' Horace then comments, ironically, **verum ... amplectitur ... hoc amat et laudat: "matronem nullam ego tango"**, 'but instead he embraces, loves and santifies himself thus: "Myself, I touch no matrons."' Horace then points out the awful consequence that can happen. **Ut quondam Marsaeus, amator Originis ille** 'as at some time Marsaeus, that founder of the race and such a lover'. (It seems more in keeping with the general context of the argument, bearing in mind Sallust's social status, that a comparison would be thus rather than assume a construction containing an hypothetical lover named 'Origo'.) **Qui patrium mimae donat ... "nil fuerit mi ... cum uxoribus ... alienis"**, saying, in effect, 'who gave his inheritance to an actress and claimed that he never interfered with other men's wives'. Horace then issues a warning. **Verum est cum mimis, est cum meretricibus ... fama malum gravius ... trahit** 'but in truth the harm it attracts to public esteem is a more serious matter with actresses than it is with prostitutes.' Horace then poses a question upon a question; **an tibi abunde personam ... quicquid ubique officit evitare?** in effect, 'is it sufficient for you to avoid playing the part of a adulterer but not to avoid that which is pursued, whatever and wherever it injures?' **Bonam deperdere famam, rem patris oblimare, malum est ubicumque** 'to lose a good reputation, to squander a patrimony, is terrible at any time.' **Quid interest in matrona, ancilla peccesne togata?** 'You may sin; what matters it whether with matron or slave girl in a tunic?

In the following lines, sixty-four to seventy-two, Horace uses, as an example, a famous scandal from the Republican past, that of Fausta, meaning 'Joy', the married daughter of Sulla, and two of her lovers, Villius and Longarenus. **Villius in Fausta Syllae gener ... nomine deceptus,** Horace repeats the ribald comment of the time, 'Villius, de facto son-in-law of Sulla, having been deceived by the name, Fausta,' **hoc miser uno ... poenas dedit usque superque quam satis est** 'this miserable one suffered continuous punishment enough and more than enough.' Horace goes on with the story gleefully, **pugnis caesus ferroque petitus, exclusus fore, cum Longarenus foret intus** 'having been beaten with the fist and assailed with cold steel, having been shut out in the forum when Longarenus penetrated inside'. It is difficult not to regard the use of an intentional pun here; Longarenus penetrating not only the walls of the Lady Fausta's house, for which the verb **penetro** would have served, but the lady herself for which the verb **foro** provides a double entendre. Certainly the use of the former would cause a metrical imbalance, unless the line was adjusted, but one so easily accomplished that it would seem that the use of the latter was deliberate. Horace then reflects on the feelings that might have been aroused in Villius. **Huic si mutonis verbis mala tanta videnti diceret haec animus: "quid vis tibi? Numquid ego a te magno prognatum deposco consule cunnum velatumque stola, mea cum conferbuit ira?"** The passage is quoted in full because it has a raw, passionate edge to it, much as though Horace speaks with personal experience of such treatment and it occurs to one that the writing of this Satire might date from the period of the Epodes, particularly 8 and 12, In effect it says, 'if such a one, facing so much evil, might utter to his libido, "What would you?

Reflect, I never demand from you, even when my passion has begun to boil, a highly born prostitute clothed in a stola." The answer given is obviously not sufficient, **Quid responderet? "magno patre nata puella est."** 'What might it reply? "The girl is a noble father's daughter."' It is difficult to read this passage without feeling that Horace, rather than playing the cynic, has had some experience of the physical and mental degradation of such a situation. Indeed, we might see echoes of Epode 8 and particularly Epode 12, where Horace is placed very much in the same situation of Villius. (See section 15)

In lines seventy to eighty-five Horace initially generalises on natural impulses as against contrived appetites that inevitably lead to excess. **At quanto meliora ... dives opis natura suae** 'But how much better nature herself advises in contending this costly physical power.' **Tu si modo recte dispensare ... immiscere** 'if you would only seek to arrange things correctly and not seek to be carried away.' **Tuo vitio rerumne labores, nil referre putas?** 'You think the things you suffer from not your problem to solve?' **Quare, ne paeniteat te, desine matronas sectarier, ... decerpere fructus.** In effect, 'cease to pursue married women; whereby you need not repent when the effort to draw down more evil pleasure is to take away enjoyment of the thing itself.' Horace then gives specific examples, **Nec magis huic inter niveos viridesque lapillos (sit licet hoc, Cerinthe, tuum) tenerum est femur aut crus rectius, atque etiam melius persaepe togatae est.** 'Also, very often a prostitute is better and as to this, no thigh or leg is softer or straighter between emeralds and pearls, (this may not be so of yours, Cerinthus.)' We must suppose here than Cerinthus was an exception to the general rule, in one particular or another. **Adde huc quod mercem sine fucis gestat, ... si quid honesti est, ... quaerit quo turpia celet.** 'Add to this, she carries about the merchandise without pretences; what she has for sale she exposes to view, nor, if she has beauty, seeks to emphasise it openly while she may conceal what is unsightly.'

The section covered by lines eighty-six to one hundred and five begins with a parable comparing the selection of a partner for the act of love with the selection of horse for purchase, a passage in which psychologists may well detect Freudian symbolism. **Regibus hic mos est, ubi equos mercantur** 'this is the caprice of princes, when they buy horses.' **Opertos inspiciunt,**

... **emptorem inducat hiantem.** 'They examine them covered ... it directs the buyer to the mouth.' **Quod pulchrae clunes, breve quod caput, ardua cervix. Hoc ille recte: ne corporis optima ... oculis ... Hypsaea caecior illa ... mala ... spectes.** In effect, 'ignore the beautiful haunches, small head and stately neck; seeing good points with a keen eye but being blind to the faults'. Then Horace directs attention to a man's attitude towards women, **"O crus, O bracchia!" Verum depugis ... pede longo est.** '"O leg, O arms" True, but she is narrow buttocked, with a large nose, short waist and is big of foot.' In other words, in the need to possess a man should not be blind to imperfection and the same rule applies to married women. **Matronae praeter faciem nil cernere possis, ... demissa veste tegentis.** In effect, 'One can only see a matron's face ... her long robe covers all else.' If, however, it is the very fact that she is another man's wife that urges you on, be prepared for difficulties, **Si interdicta petes, vallo circumdata (nam te hoc facit insanum) multae tibi tum officient res, ... plurima quae invideant pure apparere tibi rem.** A summary of which is, 'If you seek forbidden fruit that is surrounded by everyday obstacles ... countless things prevent a clear view of your desire.' Horace offers the alternative solution, **Altera, nil obstat; Cois tibi paene videre ut nudam, ... metiri possis oculo latus.** 'With the other option, no problem; in her transparent Coan silk she is almost naked for you to see, ... you can measure the figure with the eye.' Horace then, returning to the original parable, poses the question, **an tibi mavis insidias fieri pretiumque avellier ante quam mercem ostendi?** 'Or, before the merchandise is shown to you and before you take possession, would you prefer to become parted from the money?'

In lines one hundred and five to one hundred and ten, Horace makes use of a well known epigram of Callimachus, which compares the lover to a hunter. While it helps him to make his point he decides it offers no solace to the lover. **"Leporem venator ut alta in nive sectetur, positum sic tangere nolit,"** cantat et apponit **"meus est amor huic similis; nam transvolat in medio posita et fugienda captat."** '"A hunter, that in deep snow pursues hare, may decline to touch one that lies to hand," is celebrataed in song and goes on, "this is similar to my desire, it ignores what is already available and seeks to win that taking flight.' The apt comparison to his argument is quite clear, but then comes the corollary,

Hiscine versiculis speras tibi posse ... e pectore pelli? 'Do you hope that your breast will to be able to be opened by such verses and the anguish, passion and the burden of care to be lifted out?' Horace seems to be making the point that, although everyone speaks of love, it is passion that rules and that writing about it is no substitute to the satisfaction of that appetite.

From line one hundred and eleven to line one hundred and thirty four, the end of the Satire, Horace draws together his argument. On the one hand appetites exist to be satisfied, sexual or otherwise; on the other hand mankind is never satisfied with what is provided by the gods, it must elaborate and proceed to excess. First he poses a series of questions, **Nonne, cupidinibus statuat natura modum quem, ... et inane abscindere soldo?** 'Is it not better to ask what standard nature establishes for desire, ... and so divide the solid from the void?' **Num, tibi cum fauces urit sitis, aurea quaeris pocula? Num esuriens fastidis omnia praeter pavonem rhombumque?** 'When you are thirsty do you ask for a goblet of gold? When you are hungry do you disdain everything but peacock and turbot?' So much for two of the appetites; Horace questions the third. **Tument tibi cum inguina, num, si ancilla aut verna est praesto puer, impetus in quem continuo fiat, malis tentigine rumpi?** In essence, 'When your genitals become engorged and a serving maid or a house boy is at hand so that your erotic impulse can be satisfied instantly, would you rather burst with passion?'

Horace answers all of these in the first person, **Non ego: namque parabilem amo Venerem facilemque.** 'Not I: I love the pleasure that is easily procured and easily accomplished.' Distinguishing his dislikes and preferences; **Illam "post paulo," "sed pluris," "si exierit vir," Gallis** 'she, who says, "After a while," "but more," "if my husband has gone away," is for those priests that emasculate themselves.' **Hanc Philodemus ait sibi, ... est iussa venire.** 'Philodemus asserted himself that she must not cost too much and not too slow to come when she is commanded.' Having drawn a literary allusion, Horace concentrates on his own wishes. **Candida rectaque sit; munda hactenus ut neque ... dat natura videri.** Generally, 'she must be fair and straight, up to a point, but not more than nature intended.' **Haec ubi supposuit dextro corpus mihi laevum, Ilia**

et Egeria est; do nomen quodlibet illi, 'When she places her right hip under my left, she is Illia or Egeria; I give her whatever name she pleases.'

Horace finishes the Satire with a burst of breathless and hilarious verse that catches so exactly the predicament of a lover, caught by the husband in the act, that one may be forgiven for believing it a firsthand account. **Nec verior ne, dum futuo, vir rure recurrat, ianua frangatur, latret canis, undique magno pulsa domus strepitu resonet, vepallida lecto desiliat mulier, miseram se conscia clamet, cruribus haec metuat, doti deprensa, egomet mi.** 'I fear not, as I sow my seed, that a husband will return from the country, the front door be broken down, the dog bark, the house reverberate with noise, the woman pale, herself having been caught out, leaps from the marriage bed, afraid for her dowry, the wretched maid crying aloud for the safety of her legs and I, myself, for me.' Followed by the ignominious consequences, **discincta tunica fugiendum est et pede nudo, ne nummi pereant aut puga aut denique fama.** 'It is fleeing with dishevelled tunic and bare of foot lest financial ruin overtakes or public esteem or the fleshy parts of my body suffer harm.' **Deprendi miserum est: Fabio vel iudice vincam.** 'To be caught out is wretched: or with Fabius the judge, I might win.' Thus, with a final barb at Fabius, a Stoic and an adulterer, Horace concludes.

One cannot agree with the dismissive attitude of Fraenkel on this Satire. When we disentangle what Fraenkel has to say from the masses of literary comparisons and sources he attributes to this work, it amounts to him saying that the poetry is good but the content poor. 'What Horace has to say is in neither case of great value, but the manner in which he says it is masterly.' (Fraenkel - Horace, p. 80.) This is condescension on a grand scale; damning with faint praise is certainly too ineffective a form of condemnation to describe its inclusion. There are at last, in these more enlightened times, signs that we may be freeing ourselves from the intellectual tyranny that, in the past, we have allowed Greece over Rome. This commentary and analysis has tried to concentrate on what Horace himself is saying, not what it is assumed the literary heritage of Greece might have dictated to him. Fraenkel suggests invention to explain the content and thereby ignores the need for commentary on whole passages,

passages that cannot be treated thus if we are to understand what Horace is saying: presumambly because they cannot be identified to classic Greek sources. Satire I, 2 is surely a social commentary on Roman ethics and morals and attitudes to women in general. Consider the elements of this work and what we can learn from them; they are surely vignettes of a real society, not an imagined one. Tigellius and Fufidius are real people in real situations. Their likenesses have been observed throughout literary history, not only latterly by Dickens and Hogarth, but, preceding Horace, by Aristophanes, Menander, Terence and Plautus. They have never been stock characters from fiction but keenly observed contemporaries. The observation, or contempt, for social mores and fashions, such as displayed by Maltinus, Rufillius and Gargonius, the dichotomy of attitudes to those who frequent brothels and the open defiance of Cupennius are all exact reflections of a society that can be mirrored in those that have existed since Horace. The punishment of adulterers is still an open issue in contemporary society, from the strict rules of Islam to the relaxed attitudes of the Western World. That Roman society displayed the same mixed feelings should not surprise us nor should the ill-concealed joy in the narration of the sort of retribution that overtakes the transgressor. The attitudes taken by Galba and Sallust merely serve to confirm this ambivalent attitude. In choosing to illustrate his text by mentioning a scandal from the time of Sulla, Horace is pinning his view of his own contemporary Roman society with that of Republican Rome and finding little difference. This fact in itself would seriously suggest that Horace was not relying on invention but emphasising that mankind does not change in its attidues to fundamental issues. In the context of Horace and his love affairs, this work shows the social background against which they took place and the attitude of the younger Horace to their pursuit. His love poetry from thereon charts his maturer realisations.

YOUTHFUL ENDEAVOURS

INTRODUCTION

There are four love poems which apparently date from Horace's early years, subsequent to the rather angry young man of Satire 1, 2. The first, Epode 11, describes how Horace, recovering from an infatuation with Inachia, is ashamed at his boorish behaviour to his friends and asserts that he is no longer interested in writing little verses but that true love has overtaken him, making him yearn for young people, youths or maidens. However, on the rebound from Inachia, he has taken up with a certain Lyciscus, a young man as tender as a woman. He will do until love for a maiden or a youth with long flowing hair comes along.

The second, Epode 14, concerns Phrynea. a freedwoman, with whom Horace is having an affair. She is apparently very popular and Horace is greatly concerned to find that he is not the only lover that consoles the lady. His concern and jealousy is affecting his work and his output of poetry is suffering. At the peak of his misery Maecenas chances to ask what is wrong, why no poetry? In an acerbic reply, which is of course Epode 14, Horace retorts that no, he is not lazy, no, he has not forgotten how to write poetry; he is besotted by love for Phrynea who is playing around with other men and driving him to despair. He compares himself to Anacreon of old who, when besotted by the youth Bathyllus, was likewise affected. With this example, and an abrupt volte-face, Horace metaphorically turns the tables on Maecenas by saying that he, Maecenas, is in danger of being burnt by love's fires and that even if it be sweet at the moment, he should enjoy it while it lasts. This is the reference to Maecenas having a very torrid affair with a young Greek actor, also named Bathyllus, with whom Maecenas became so infatuated that he apparently lost all sense of proportion and his friends became very worried about his health and sanity.

Epode 15 is about Neaera, who swore eternal fidelity to Horace and then betrayed him regularly with a rival. Horace swears to find another love, more fitting and more true and will never look at Neaera ever again. To his rival he gives warning that though he might have all the material, sartorial and physical advantages over Horace, his turn will come and Horace will laugh last. Horace uses metaphor, first from nature, to signify the love he thought he shared with Nearea, and latterly, from the Greek myths, to paint a picture of his rival's wealth and standing in the community. It is unique in that Horace names himself within the poem: calling himself Flaccus he declares that he has had enough of the lady.

Ode 5 from Book I is the famous Pyrrha ode of which, it is said, more translations exist than of the remainder of Horace's poetry put together. It fully deserves that attention. It is Horace caught very much on the raw edge of emotion; Pyrrha would seem to have hurt him deeply. It gives us a close insight into Roman sexual practices and the name Pyrrha for instance is not thought to be a normal Roman descriptive cognomen but more epithetical in nature. At first it is possible to assume that it is a sexual connotation, more or less 'hot stuff', but later it would seem that it probably refers to temper and 'fiery' would be a more accurate interpretation. Again the verb describing the act of love itself hardly has connotations of a leisurely affair; *urgeo* suggests a more abandoned form of such activity. The venue of the coupling is clearly a grotto and rose petals form the couch on which the action takes place and this, with the later reference to the god of the sea, could very well indicate the form of the grotto that later became notorius under Tiberius. Constructed within the grounds of a villa, such a grotto contained pools and fountains in which statues of Neptune, Venus, Thetis and sea creatures featured largely and whose purpose, beside providing cool relief from the sun, seemed to have been to stimulate sexual appetites towards debauchery. Horace uses no invective in this poem but kills with kind words. The lady is all golden but uncomfortably superficial it seems; she is calm mirrored perfection until she is crossed; she is jewel-like, glittering but hard; she is exciting to be with but treacherous. Horace closes with the admission that he is still ensnared, remembering the mad infatuation that also caused him to lose his senses in that same grotto.

EPODE 11

Petti, nihil me sicut antea iuvat
Scribere versiculos amore percussum gravi,
Amore, qui me praeter omnes expetit
Mollibus in pueris aut in puellis urere.
Hic tertius December, ex quo destiti
Inachia furere, silvis honorem decutit.
Heu me, per urbem, nam pudet tanti mali,
Fabula quanta fui! Conviviorum et paenitet,
In quis amantem languor et silentium
Arguit et latere petitus imo spiritus.
"contrane lucrum nil valere candidum
Pauperis ingenium!" querebar adplorans tibi,
Simul calentis inverecundus deus
Fervidiore mero arcana promorat loco.
"Quod si meis inaestuet praecordiis
Libera bilis, ut haec ingrata ventis dividat
Fomenta, vulnus nil malum levantia,
Desinet imparibus certare summotus pudor."
Ubi haec severus te palam laudaveram,
Iussus abire domum ferebar incerto pede
Ad non amicos heu mihi postis et heu
Limina dura, quibus lumbos et infregi latus.
Nunc gloriantis quamlibet mulierculam
Vincere mollitia amor Lycisci me tenet;
Unde expedire non amicorum queant
Libera consilia nec contumeliae graves,
Sed alius ardor aut puellae candidae
Aut teretis pueri, longam renodantis comam.

INACHIA

Pettius, it pleases me no longer, as before, to write
Small verse about love, having been stricken so as
To be burdened, by love, which beyond all seeks to
Burn me with passion for sweet youths and maidens.
This third December, since when I shook off passion
For Inachia, shakes off the glory from the woods.
Alas, it shames me, how much I have been the subject
Of malicious gossip around the city! I repent the
Social occasions in which silence and languor proved
Infatuation; to conceal the sighing brought forth
"A poor man's natural talents prove to be worthless
Against dazzling wealth!" I was always complaining to
You, lamenting, once the impudent God's fiery, neat
Wine had warmed and brought forth from secret places.
"What if unbridled anger may boil within my breast so
As to disperse these thankless fomentations to the
Four winds, for not relieving the cowardly injustice,
Modesty will cease to struggle, defeated by inequality"
When I had praised this stern action in your presence and
Having been ordered to go home I was being helped away on
Uncertain foot alas to a door post unfriendly to me and
Alas, hard steps against which I dashed my side and loins.
Love from a little woman holds me now, of Lyciscus, boastfully
Claiming, if you please, to hold mastery over tenderness;
From whom no altruistic counsels and neither stern reproaches
From friends will be able to disentangle, but only another
Burst of passion, either from glittering, nubile maidens
Or from well rounded youths, with long, free flowing hair.

EPODE 14

Mollis inertia cur tantam diffuderit imis
Oblivionem sensibus,

Pocula Lethaeos ut si ducentia somnos
arente fauce traxerim,

Candide Maecenas, occidis saepe rogando:
Deus, deus nam me vetat

Inceptos, olim promissum carmen, iambos
Ad umbilicum adducere.

Non aliter Samio dicunt arsisse Bathyllo
Anacreonta Teium,

Qui persaepe cava testudine flevit amorem
Non elaboratum ad pedem.

Ureris ipse miser: quod si non pulchrior ignis
Accendit obsessam Ilion,

Gaude sorte tua; me libertina, nec uno
Contenta, Phryne macerat.

PHRYNE

*You torment me, steadfast Maecenas, by asking
Many times why so great*

*An aversion to work has so diffused oblivion
Over my creative senses*

*As if, thirsty, I had drained the Letharean cup.
The same God forbids me*

*Begin, while also promising iambic metre to bring
Full circle to the Ode.*

*Phryne, a freedwoman, not content with a single
Lover, burns me. They say*

*That thus Teian Anacreon burned for Samian Bathyllus
And often lamented love,*

*Elaborating simple metre on Tortoise-shell Lyre. You
Yourself are so burnt, unhappy*

*One; in the hope that flame be not so fair as burned steady Troy
Rejoice in your fortune.*

EPODE 15

Nox erat et caelo fulgebat Luna sereno
Inter minora sidera,

Cum tu, magnorum numen laesura deorum,
In verba iurabas mea,

Artius atque hedera procera adstringitur ilex
Lentis adhaerens bracchiis,

Dum pecori lupus et nautis infestus Orion
Turbaret hibernum mare,

Intonsoque agitaret Apollinis aura capillos,
Fore hunc amorem mutuum.

O dolitura mea multum virtute Neaera!
nam si quid in Flacco viri est,

Non feret adsiduas potiori te dare noctes,
Et quaeret iratus parem;

Nec semel offensi cedet constantia formae,
Si certus intrarit dolor.

Et tu, quicumque es felicior atque meo nunc
Superbus incedis malo,

Sis pecore et multa dives tellure licebit
Tibique Pactolus fluat,

Nec te Pythagorae fallant arcana renati,
Formaque vincas Nirea,

Eheu, translato alio maecrebis amores.
Ast ego vicissim risero.

NEAERA

Night, and in a serene sky the moon was incandescent
Amidst the fainter stars,

When you, about to flout the name of the great Gods
Were swearing your solemn oath,

While long limbs were binding us together as the Ivy
Makes flexible arms to the Oak,

As long as the wolf is hostile to cattle and Orion
With stormy seas, to sailors,

The breeze stir the hair of Apollo's unshorn head
Then so long this love of ours.

O Neaera, about to suffer much grief from my resolve
For if there is any manhood in Flaccus,

He will not bear others to possess and you to give
Nightly, but will angrily seek another.

Nor, once suffered offence will he yield his purpose
If stern anger has entered him.

And you, whosoever you are, happier and also proud
Now that you exult over my distress

You may be rich with many cattle and plentiful estates,
And Pactolus may flow for you,

Nor the magic of Pythagoras be hidden but rise again for you
And you may surpass Nireus in looks,

Alas you too will mourn affections given to another
I, on the other hand, will laugh in turn.

ODES I, 5

Quis multa gracilis te puer in rosa
Perfusus liquidis urget odoribus
Grato, Pyrrha, sub antro?
Cui flavam religas comam,

Simplex munditiis?   Heu quotiens fidem
Mutatosque deos flebit et aspera
Nigris aequora ventis
Emirabitur insolens,

Qui nunc te fruitur credulus aurea,
Qui semper vacuam, semper amabilem
Sperat, nescius aurae
Fallacis.   Miseri, quibus

Intemptata nites.   Me tabula sacer
Votiva paries indicat uvida
Suspendisse potenti
Vestimenta maris deo.

PYRRHA

What slender youth, upon a bed with many rose petals
And perfumed with sweet smelling liquids, makes love
To you now, Pyrrha, within the welcoming grotto?
For whom do you arrange your hair, so golden.

So simple. So elegant.   Hah!   How often will he be
Amazed when black and angry winds roughen the calm
Surface and he will lament changed fidelity
And indeed, changed Gods.

Who now delights in you easily believing the gold is
Real, who expects constant availability, constant
Amiability, unaware of the treacherous
Breath of favour.   Yet to be pitied, they,

Not having experienced your brilliance. Within that
Same grotto, a sacred tablet vowing vestments to the
God of the Sea, records the drunken
Power you must have held over me.

ANALYSIS & COMMENTARY

EPODE 11

Lines one to ten which form the opening of this Epode find Horace in a very depressed state of mind, protesting that desire for love itself prevents him from writing any poetry at all. Regrets for an old infatuation make him dull company and a concern to his friends. **Petti, nihil ... iuvat scribere ... percussum gravi.** In effect, 'Pettius, having been stricken so as to be burdened by love, it pleases me no longer to write verses.' Horace then elaborates on his desire, **amore, qui me praeter omnes expetit mollibus in pueris aut in puellis urere.** 'By love, which, beyond all things, seeks to burn me with passion for delectable youths and maidens.' He then relapses into nostalgic brooding, **hic tertius December ... destiti Inachia ... silvis honorem decutit.** 'This, the third December since I shook off desire for Inachia, shakes off the glory from the woods.' Ruefully and then sorrowfully, **heu me, per urbem, ... fabula quanta fui!** 'Alas, it makes me ashamed how much an object of gossip I have been around the city!' **Conviviorum et paenitet, ... languor et silentium ... latere petitus imo spiritus.** 'I repent having sought languor and silence on social occasions to conceal the infatuation, yes and even the sigh which proved it.'

Lines ten to twenty-two see Horace reacting against this depression with an amusing account of himself in the thrall of it; quite under the influence of wine, belligerent, jocose and unsteady on his legs. **"Contrane lucrum nil valere candidum pauperis ingenium!" querebar adplorans tibi.** 'I was always complaining, lamenting to you, "to avail against wealth, the honest disposition of a poor man is as nothing."' **Simil calentis ... fervidiore mero ... loco.** 'As soon as the impudent God, Bacchus, had warmed with fiery wine it had brought forth from a secret hiding place.' **"Quod si meis inaestuet praecordiis libera bilis, ... desinet imparibus certare summotus pudor."** 'What if righteous anger, easing not the grievous wound, should boil within my breast in such a way that might scatter to the winds such thankless fomentations; modesty, having been compelled to give up, will cease to struggle with unequals.' **Ubi haec severus te palam laudaveram, ... ferebar incerto pede ad non amicos ... limina dura ... lumbos et infregi latus.** 'When I had sternly extolled this to you publicly, having been

- 60 -

commanded to go home I was being borne away with uncertain foot towards, alas for me, an unfriendly door post and, alas, a hard threshold, against which I knocked my loins and side.'

In lines twenty-three to twenty-eight, Horace admits to a liaison with another man, as a temporary remedy, heedless to the advice of friends. He waits until a more permanent love comes along. **Nunc gloriantis quamlibet mulierculam vincere mollitia amor Lycisci me tenet;** 'Love of Lyciscus, ever so much a little woman, boasting to master tenderness, detains me now;' **Unde expedire non amicorum queant ... sed alius ardor ... aut puellae ... longam renodantis coman.** 'From whom no unsolicited counsels nor stern reproaches can hope to set me free but only another passionate love either from dazzling young women or graceful youth, with free flowing hair.'

This is a work from the early years of Horace and if it surprises us by its candid content, we should try to understand that he lived in a society which, in its social pretentions at least, tended to copy that of the golden age of Greece and Sparta. Therefore we should assume that its attitude to bisexual and homosexual behaviour mirrored those earlier societies, even if it was more the case of public utterance as against private belief. From the Satire I, 2, we learn that he advocates taking one's pleasures with whichever sex may be willing and available. Yet there is a distinct feeling that he is out to shock his readers in the last six lines. Whether this is youthful bravado or matter of fact comment is hard to determine. Certainly it is written on the rebound from Inachia and the bitterness of that rejection is very apparent. In such circumstances lovers are prone to move to extremes.

Fraenkel's comment, 'Epode XI ... is an elegant piece of writing but there is little real life in it' (Fraenkel Horace 67) tends to move one to a greater despair than even Horace shows.

EPODE 14

This sixteen line Epode can be regarded as being of two equal parts; the first eight lines being a rhetorical reply to criticism by Maecenas, the second eight lines drawing classical allusions and containing a pointed reference to Maecenas's own love life. Horace is in love again and it is again affecting his poetical output. He pleads his case to Maecenas and suggests there are classical precedents, completing the Epode with an elegant version of the aphorism on the pot calling the kettle black. The introduction to the Epode actually begins with line five, then proceeds from line one through to line eight where it picks up line fifteen point five and sixteen then completes from line nine through to line fifteen point four. Horace asks, plaintively, **Candide Maecenas, occidis saepe rogando:** 'Sincere Maecenas, you torment me by asking repeatedly,'. **Mollis inertia cur tantam ... oblivionem sensibus** 'Why so great an aversion to work has diffused indolent forgetfulness over my subconscious senses'. He then elaborates, referring to the mythical river Lethe that runs through Hades, a drink from whose water brings instant forgetfulness of the past. **Pocula Lethaeos ut si ... traxerim,** 'as if with throat, languishing from thirst, I had drained the cup that leads to Lethean sleep'. Stating his dilemma, **Deus, deus nam me vetat incepto ... ad umbilicum adducere.** 'The God promising iambic metre for me to bring full circle to my Ode, is the same God that forbids I begin.' Horace explains what has happened to him, **me libertina, nec uno contenta, Phryne macerat .** 'The freedwoman Phryne, not content with one man, tortures me.'

Horace then quotes the example of the classical Greek poet, Anacreon, who suffered similarly. **Non aliter Samio dicunt arsisse Bathyllo Anacreonta Teium,** 'They do say it was no different when Anacreon of Teius was on fire for Bathyllus of Samos.' So, Horace asserts, did his work. **Qui persaepe ... elaboratum ad pedem** 'who very often lamented his love to a tortoise shell lyre, elaborating to a simple metre'. Horace then returns to the present with a barbed remark to Maecenas, referring to Maecenas's current lover, also named Bathyllus. **Ureris ipse miser:** 'You, yourself are being burnt by love's fire, unhappy one': Then, relenting a little, but with a final elegant flip of literary wit, he returns to classical allusion and to the flame that was Helen's beauty, setting fire to Paris and, of course, Troy itself. **quod si non pulchrior ignis ... obsessam Ilion, gaude sorte tua:** 'in the hope that the flame is not more beautiful than that which burned down besieged Troy, rejoice in your fortune.'

Fraenkel is a little more forthcoming on this Epode but still groping a little for lack of a distinct literary hook into Greek classicism. He seizes avidly on the mention of Anacreon, mentions Catullus briefly in passing and grudgingly agrees that here, Horace might well have done his own thing. This 'thing' however, is revealed as a rather marvellous piece of poetry, elegant, witty, self deprecating and deliciously sarcastic. The tongue-in-cheek line about the effect of Helen on Troy and Bathyllus being too hot for Maecenas to handle, must be one of the most biting couplets in the history of literature.

EPODE 15

This Epode divides logically into three sections. In the first section, lines one to ten, Horace accepts the assurances of love and constancy from Neaera, despite misgivings. In the second section, lines eleven to sixteen Horace berates himself for being such a fool and vows to find another love. In the third section, lines seventeen to twenty-four, Horace addresses his rival telling him that he, in his turn, will be treated in just the same fashion.

The first section of this Epode has a most evocative opening, **Nox erat et caelo fulgebat Luna sereno inter minora sidera,** 'It was night and in the serene heavens the moon was glittering between the less bright stars.' Horace asks that his beloved pledge her love, **Cum tu, magnorem numen laesura deorum, in verba iurabas mea** 'when you, about to offend against the name of the great Gods, were swearing an oath in my words'. Horace describes the embrace in which she betarys him, **Artius ... adstringitur ... adhaerens bracchiis** 'Long slender arms binding together more closely than the flexible ivy adheres to the holm oak'. Then the words he asked her to swear were true for ever, **Dum pecori lupus ... Orion turbaret hibernum mare, intonsosque agitaret Apollinis aura capillos, fore hunc amorem mutuum** 'while the wolf is hostile to cattle and Orion stirs up the wintry sea for sailors, while the unshorn locks of Apollo's hair might be stirred by the motion of air, then so long this love of ours'.

The second section begins with a cry of vengeance, **O dolitura mea multum virtute Neaera!** 'O Neaera, about to suffer much pain from my resolution!' Horace, having found out about his rival, issues the anguished cry of betrayed lovers throughout the ages. **Nam si quid in Flacco viri est, non feret adsiduas potiori, te dare noctes** 'For, in the hope that there is anything of a man in Flaccus.' followed by the ineffective threat, **et**

quaeret iratus parem 'and, having been made angry, will seek another just as beautiful'. Underlining the threat that there will be no reprieve, **nec semel offensi cedet constantia formae, si certus intrarit dolor** 'nor, once you have offended constancy, if determined animosity may have entered in, will it yield to beauty.'

In the third section, Horace addresses the other man. **Et tu, quicumque es ... superbus incedis malo** 'And you, whosoever you are, proud and happy, that now triumph over my misfortune'. Horace lists the assumed attractions of his rival, **Sis pecore et multa dives ... Pactolus fluat ... Pythagorae fallant ... formaque vincas Nirea** 'you may be rich in lands and many cattle, Pactolus may be permitted to flow for you, the secrets of Pythagoras to rise up again and deceive you not and you may surpass the beauty of Nireus'. Thus Horace mockingly equips the new paramour with the riches of this world and the mythical riches of the classical past; Pactolus, the river of Lydia with sands of gold, the unknown secrets of Pythagoras, killed at Syracuse before he had lived a full life and Nireus, said to be the most handsome man at the siege of Troy. However, he warns, **Eheu, translatos alio maerebis amores. Ast ego vicissim risero** 'Alas, you will mourn loves transferred to another. I, on the other hand, will laugh in turn.'

Fraenkel is more comfortable with this Epode and feels that it owes much to Hellenistic origins. He notes its jealousy and acrimony, attributing them elsewhere but he does not comment at all on this work as poetry in its own right. The theme of love, betrayal, jealousy and vindictive feelings is universal certainly but Horace's magnificent poetical treatment deserves some applause. It certainly does not merit being bound and gagged by the tendrils of classical literature.

BOOK I, ODE 5

This Ode divides, thematically, into three sections. Line one to line five point five poses certain questions, line five point six to line twelve point four lists certain consequences arising therefrom and line twelve point five to line sixteen is a reflection on past events. The voice is that of an erstwhile lover jealously contemplating the delights his successor is experiencing and cynically predicting his probable fate. At the same time he is experiencing his own onetime joy, disillusionment and final rejection.

Horace, who is the former lover, begins with a plaintive question, **Quis ... gracilis te puer ... urget ... Pyrrha** 'Pyrrha, what slender youth presses down upon you.' It is clear that the verb refers to the act of love but the use of the strong verb <u>urgeo</u> implies something more energetic than casual love making. One might therefore query the use of <u>puer</u> where one might expect <u>amator</u>. Young, strong and virile are naturally conjured up by its use but whether it implies a house slave and thereby, to use the Edwardian vernacular, 'a bit of rough trade', is open to question. It certainly seems to imply a preference for energetic ecounters on the part of the lady concerned. Horace paints the well remembered surroundings of the embrace, **multa ... in rosa perfusus liquidis ... odoribus** 'upon many rose petals and perfumed with sweet smelling oils' This brilliant descriptive passage sets a luxurious scene and places, for the mind, the image of the gleaming, interlocked bodies, engendered by the first statement, into an atmosphere heavy with perfume and placed upon a counterpane brightly coloured by rose petals. Horace now describes where the encounter will have taken place, **grato ... sub antro** 'within the welcome grotto'. Somewhere sheltered seems to be implied and, bearing in mind the climate of central Italy, somewhere cool. It is unlikely that a rural setting is implied also since, by the time of Tiberius, a grotto, either natural or artificially constructed, was the feature of many villas. Complete with pools of water and fountains, it supplied a welcome relief from the climate. By the archaeological evidence from the time of Tiberius the grotto seems to have been dedicated to Neptune, Thetis and the divinities of the sea in general. This idea may well have existed well before that time and explain the reference in this Ode. Horace now switches to the lady's appearance, **cui flavam religas comam, simplex munditiis?** 'For whom do you arrange your hair, so golden. so simple. so elegant?' Following on from such a vivid descriptive passage, this question might well be intended to increase the erotic image already given, by presenting the lady, while engaged in abandoned love-making, as immaculately groomed and elegant. However, it is essentially a pivotal phrase since it leads on into the next passage where Pyrrha is shown to be, potentially, anything but calm, elegant and mundane.

Horace now turns upon his successor with a cry of anger, and mockingly addresses him in the third person, **heu quotiens ... emirabitur**, 'Hah! How often will he be amazed.' A fierce snort, such as Hah! is to be preferred here rather than a plaintive Alas, since what follows is a remembered catalogue of Pyrrha's faults. **... Et aspera nigris aequora ventis ... insolens** 'when black and angry winds roughen the calm surface.' This passage depends on the pivotal phrase, <u>simplex munditiis</u> for its effect, Horace using the simile of calm water suddenly lashed by a gale to reveal the sudden burst of temper that can emanate from Pyrrha. Horace pities his rival and predicts the effect that such outbursts will have, **fidem mutatosque deos flebit** 'he will lament changed fidelity and indeed, changed Gods.' A much more elegant way of saying 'he will wonder where love has gone and what hit him'. Next, Horace cynically describes the false sense of euphoria that presently exists in the mind of the young man.

Qui nunc te fruitur credulus aurea, 'who now delights in your company, believing in all you say and what you appear to be', implying possibly, that because the golden hair is not real, the lady is counterfeit all through. He continues, **qui semper vacuam, semper amabilem sperat** 'who expects you to be always available to him alone, always pleasant to be with'. There is a biting edge to this passage; Horace himself fell into the same trap. Explaining the gullibility of men with a beautiful play on the words <u>aurea</u> - gold and <u>aurae</u> - a zephyr of wind, soon gone. **Nescius aurae fallacis,** 'Not knowing the treacherous breeze of her favours'.

Horace, having spoken his mind to his rival, now becomes introspective. **Miseri, quibus intemptata nites** 'But, to be pitied, they not having experienced the brilliance.' Here, Horace admits that, despite everything that has happened, he would not have foregone his affair with Pyrrha. One knows the feeling all too well! He now remembers the foolish things he did for love of her. **Tabula sacer votiva paries ... vestimenta maris deo** 'In that same grotto there hangs a sacred tablet, vowing vestments to the God of the Sea.' The grotto, containing as it has been proved by excavation, statues of the marine deities, would be regarded as a quasi-temple. Despite its use for amorous purposes it would be a natural place for a lover, charged with the emotion of the moment, to hang a votive tablet. Just as naturally to dedicate it to Neptune, or better still, Aphrodite in remembrance of his own beloved. Vowing vestments to adorn the statue of a God was a commonplace occurence. Horace now ends with a volte face giving us a delicious joke at his own expense. **Me ... indicat uvida suspendisse potenti ...** 'Records the drunken power that you held over me.' The joke is, of course, that the marine deities are always depicted without vestments at all, that state being common to their natural environment. The implication is that anyone vowing vestments to them must therefore be completely out of their mind. It is not supposed that this actually happened; it is sufficient for Horace to suggest that he was capable of doing such a thing. It is in the mould of kind of dry, offbeat humour that is self-deprecating, self-revealing and quite devastating in its impact.

This Ode needs to be experienced as well as read; the images are so vivid. So vivid that any reader who has been in love will recognise the inherent emotion. To anyone who has loved deeply and subsequently lost that love, the message must be quite poignant. Fraenkel does not mention this Ode at all in his commentaries. Quinn sees the emphasis as being placed rather more on the participants than on the observer, as though Horace is neutral and commenting on a situation that is remote from him. This is surely only a valid argument if one accepts the premise that Horace wrote love poetry at second hand, sublimating theory for practice.

The four works comprising this section date from Horace's youth and therefore might well represent early experiences in love. In Epodes 11 and 14, Horace is seen to be established as a poet and, in 14 at least, already under the patronage of Maecenas. His wry comments on his social status in Epode 15 lead us to believe that he had not yet acquired his villa near Tiburnus. Ode I, 5 is also assumed to date from the same time. The general feeling is that Horace is experimenting with love, homosexual and heterosexual and still finding his own level of acceptable experience. Certainly, from this time until shortly before his death, when he is in his fifties, there are no further references to love affairs with men. We must presume, from the succession of names in his middle life, that he opted for heterosexual affairs.

LYDIA

LYDIA

The four Odes about Lydia cover an unknown space of time since, in them, she progresses from a young girl to an older woman, although old in this poetical context may mean no longer attractive, desirable or even fashionable. The attitude of the poet to Lydia ranges from open admiration through besotted infatuation to an apparent cruel sarcasm and on to a final reconciliation. In form they differ greatly, much in keeping with the general feeling engendered by each poem. Was Lydia a real person? Was Horace her lover? Is it the same woman throughout? Reading the four Odes in sequence, one is made aware of an underlying thread of consciousness that one is indeed reading about the same person, as much by Horace's own attitude to her as by any persona that emerges from the text. As for Horace's personal involvement with her, there is also the feeling of a carefully controlled mixture of despair and joy in her company, that emanates from his words. In all, one is left with the certainty that Horace is describing a true emotional passage in his life, a passage where he was racked by feelings of love for this attractive woman.

Lydia is first encountered through Horace's eyes by her effect on his friend, Sybaris, whose masculine pursuits are completely diverted by her charms. Horace plaintively asks her what has happened to his friend. Where once he had a adventurous companion he now no longer sees him around his old haunts. We gain a background of the pursuits of young men of the leisured class in Imperial Rome and although there are some strange references, in general the picture is that of the same devastating effect of first love on a young man that pertains today. Lydia is next encountered as the mistress of Horace himself and Horace displays all the vulnerability of a man in love with a woman, uncertain of his hold and conscious of the envy of others and their desire to possess what he considers to be his. The two feelings that emanate from this poem are that Horace is much older than Lydia and that he feels himself at a disadvantage, not only because of this but because of his own physical imperfections, real or imaginary. The poem ends with platitudes on love, constancy and togetherness but with the overall feeling tha Horace is fooling only himself.

At first sight the third poem on Lydia seems cruel and one assumes that Horace is taking revenge. Lydia is painted as living a lonely life, shunned by men and not even attracting the attention of bawdy youth. It is a savage reversal of Horace's concern where once, in the middle poem, it was precisely this attention that drove him to jealousy. However, careful inspection reveals that neither Lydia's age nor her circumstances are what they seem! The fourth poem is an amusing reconciliation between old adversaries. Both have new partners, in Horace's case it is Chloe, both, it seems, would die for their new love but above all, both would like to return to the old days when they lived only for each other. While it is last in the sequence of four, its general feeling would place it third, since Horace's Ode to the older Lydia seems so final. However, love being what it is, who knows? Taken as a group, these poems display a virtuosity in conveying emotion by sheer poetical craftmanship. The word content, the rhythmic form and the overall impact of the invidual poems convey a life- like Lydia, her disturbing beauty in the first two, the abyss of feeling that the passing of that beauty engenders in the third and the air of teasing playfulness in the fourth. One cannot invent a three dimensional woman such as Lydia from the recesses of a purely objective imagination however much aesthetic creativity is applied. If Lydia is not a real person then Horace had a model in mind; if his emotion was not lavished specifically on her, it already had been lavished on someone else. These are undoubtedly poems born of experience.

ODES I, 8

Lydia, dic. per omnes
Te deos oro, Sybarin cur properes amando
Perdere; cur apricum
Oderit campum, patiens pulveris atque solis;

Cur neque militaris
Inter aequales equitet. Gallica nec lupatis
Temperet ora frenis.
Cur timet flavum Tiberim tangere? cur olivum

Sanguine viperino
Cautius vitat, neque iam livida gestat armis
Bracchia, saepe disco,
Saepe trans finem iaculo nobilis expedito?

Quid latet, ut marinae
Filium dicunt Thetidis sub lacrimosa Troiae
Funera, ne virilis
Cultus in caedem et Lycias proriperet catervas?

LYDIA - IN HER YOUTH

Lydia, by all the gods
I beg, say why you are hurrying Sybaris to ruin
With love, why has he,
Once so tolerant of sun and dust forsaken the campus

Why no longer rides
Amongst his cavalry cronies, nor controls the Gallic
Mount with sharp bridle
Why fears he the touch of murky Tiber? Why avoid

Olive oil more cautiously
Than viper's blood, nor now exult in forearm bruised
From weapon drill, renowned
For discus and javelin, easily across the boundary?

Why hide, as they say did the son of
Thetis, Sea Goddess, when piteous Troy was doomed to
Dreadful death, lest his habit
Of male attire, bring him to death at Lycian hands?

ODES I, 13

Cum tu, Lydia, Telephi
Cervicem roseam, cerea Telephi
Laudas bracchia, vae, meum
Fervens difficili bile tumet iecur.

Tunc nec mens mihi nec color
Certa sede manet, umor et in genas
Furtim labitur, arguens
Quam lentis penitus macerer ignibus.

Uror, seu tibi candidos
Turparunt umeros immodicae mero
Rixae, sive puer furens
Impressit memorem dente labris notam.

Non, si me satis audias,
Speres perpetuum dulcia barbare
Laedentem oscula, quae Venus
Quinta parte sui nectaris imbuit.

Felices ter et amplius
Quos inrupta tenet copula nec malis
Divulsus querimoniis
Suprema citius solvet amor die.

LYDIA - IN HER PRIME

O Lydia, when you praise the nape
Of Telephus's rosy neck, the smooth waxen skin
Of Telephus's forearm, alas, my impetuous
Liver boils with passion and with dangerous bile.

Then, for me, neither my feelings
Nor my composure, stay unchanged and tears steathily
Begin to form in eyelids, proving
With what glowing internal fires I may be consumed.

I burn whether some brawl made hot
With unmixed wine, has defiled your chaste shoulders
Or whether this wild, drunken youth
Has marked with teeth, lasting imprints on your lip.

Enough, if you will listen to me
From one who would so savagely hurt the sweet little
Mouth Venus has moistened with a fifth
Part of her nectar, you may not expect constancy.

Three times, and more, happy
They whose bond holds fast nor incompatible feelings
Break up by stupid quarrels
Until love unloosens when the final day is reached.

ODES I, 25

Parcius iunctas quatiunt fenestras
Ictibus crebris iuvenes protervi,
Nec tibi somnos adimunt, amatque
Ianua limen,

Quae prius multum facilis movebat
Cardines. Audis minus et minus iam:
"me tuo longas pereunte noctes,
Lydia, dormis?"

Invicem moechos anus arrogantes
Flebis in solo levis angiportu,
Thracio bacchante magis sub inter-
Lunia vento,

Cum tibi flagrans amor et libido,
Quae solet matres furiare equorum,
Saeviet circa iecur ulcerosum,
Non sine questu,

Laeta quod pubes hedera virenti
Gaudeat pulla magis atque myrto,
Aridas frondes hiemis sodali
Dedicet Euro

LYDIA - GROWING OLD

*Seldom are groups of youths impudently
Shaking your shutters with repeated blows,
Nor is sleep taken away, the outer door
Loves the threshold*

*That once moved so often and so easily upon
The hinges. Less and less now you hear:
"Lydia, you sleep, the long nights waste away
And I for you."*

*In turn you will lament the arrogance of lovers
An insignificant woman alone in a narrow street,
More a bacchante than the Thracian wind before
The crescent moon,*

*When for you, burning love and violent desire
That, more in keeping with furious mares in heat,
Will rage around your liver so wounded by love,
Not without lament,*

*That joyful youth rejoices far more in green ivy
And also in dark green myrtle and will surrender
Old and withered foliage to Winter's companion,
The East Wind.*

ODES III, 9

"Donec gratus eram tibi
Nec quisquam potior bracchia candidae
Cervici iuvenis dabat,
Persarum vigui rege beatior."

    "Donec non alia magis
    Arsisti neque erat Lydia post Chloen,
    Multi Lydia nominis
    Romana vigui clarior Ilia."

"Me nunc Thressa Chloe regit
Dulces docta modos et citharae sciens,
Pro qua non metuam mori,
Si parcent animae fata superstiti."

    "Me torret face mutua
    Thurini Calais filius Ornyti,
    Pro quo bis patiar mori,
    Si parcent puero fata superstiti."

"Quid si prisca redit Venus
Diductosque iugo cogit aeneo?
Si flava excutitur Chloe
Reiectaeque patet ianua Lydiae?"

    "Quamquam sidere pulchrior
    Ille est, tu levior cortice et improbo
    Iracundior Hadria,
    Tecum vivere amem, tecum obeam libens!"

LYDIA - RECONCILIATION

"So long as I was pleasing to you
Nor some better youth was throwing his arms
About your beautiful neck
I thrived more content than the Persia's king."

    "So long as for no other you were
    Burning more and it was not Lydia after Chloe
    I, Lydia, flourished in name
    Much more brilliantly than Roman Ilia."

"Thracian Chloe rules me now,
Knowing the lyre and experienced in delicate melodies,
I shall not be afraid to die before,
If the Fates will spare the life to be continued on."

    "Calais, son of Thurian Ornytus
    Burns me with the torch of reciprocal love,
    For whom I will endure to die twice,
    If the Fates will spare the boy to live on."

"What if erstwhile love returns again
And collects her separated lovers under a brazen yoke?
If golden yellow Chloe is thrown out
And to rejected Lydia the door lies wide open?"

    "Although he is more beautiful than
    The stars, you are more trifling than that cork and
    More inclined to anger that the wild Adriatic,
    With you I would love to live, with you gladly die"

ANALYSIS & COMMENTARY

ODES I, 8.

The Ode to Lydia in her youth, is a cascade of questions which can all be completed with the same obvious answer. They are posed as allusions to the interrupted pursuits of her lover Sybaris. **- Cur properes ... perdere? - cur ... oderit campum? - cur neque ... equitet? - cur timet ... Tiberim? cur olivum ... vitat? - Quid latet?** Love of Lydia is the obvious answer and the interrupted pursuits are those of a young Roman male undergoing the required military training after assuming the *toga virilis*. By which we may assume that Sybaris is between fifteen and seventeen years of age. The age of Lydia is problematical but the assumption of similar youthfulness is a charitable gesture.

amando sits more comfortably in translation as an ablative noun, 'with love' suiting the metrical context and English syntax better than the alternative 'with loving'.

Apricum campum 'the open field', contrasted with **patiens pulveris ... solis** 'suffering dust and sun', allows a compression in translation. Suffering is not really implied and tolerance can be assumed, while the open field is known to be the barrack square.

Militaris inter aequales implies cavalry exercises as a company rather than an individual; **Gallica ... frenis** implies the necessary training to control the Gallic cavalry horse to command amongst a mass of others, rather than a riding lesson.

Flavum ... tangere 'yellow coloured' or 'murky' and 'to touch'. Swimming in the Tiber is implied, either in training or for pleasure. Whether the river is coloured by the spring thaws or by the effluent from the Roman sewerage system is equally unclear; the former would be a seasonal, the latter a constant, peril. In either event, the present infinitive **tangere**, 'to touch' falls better as a substantive, 'the touch', in translation.

Sanguine viperino cautius 'more cautiously than viper's blood', implies the belief that a snake's blood also contains its venom and its mere touch on skin with open wounds would be fatal. Olive oil was used in athletics, particularly wrestling, part of military training. **Neque ... bracchia** 'nor exults in bruised arms' picks up the viper's blood motif while **saepe ... expedito** underlines the athletic prowess required of a young Roman male.

Ut marinae filium dicunt Thetidis 'as they say the son of the Sea Goddess Thetis'. The son of the Sea Goddess Thetis was of course Achilles; **sub lacrimosa Troiae funera,** 'before the piteous deaths of Troy' the culmination of all the deaths, including his own, at Troy. Achilles is said to have remained hidden to avoid going to the Trojan War but both he and Troy were doomed by the Gods from the beginning. The context of this line is therefore that one cannot avoid one's fate and that since love of Lydia is decreed for Sybaris, remaining hidden will not save him. The comparison is heavy but in keeping with the mock seriousness of the whole piece. **Ne virilis cultus** 'lest the habit of male attire', is an unintended pun while **in caedem ... catervas?**, 'bring him death by Lycian troops of soldiers' closes the comparisons. Quinn suggests that **virilis cultus** might be strengthened in translation to have the meaning 'playing the part of a man', as a reference to the post-puberty appetite of a young male. If so, **caedem ... catervas** is a little strong as a corollary and it is doubtful if Horace intended this. As with most of the love poetry of Horace, Fraenkel has nothing to say on this, or any of the other Lydia Odes.

ODE I, 13

The first two stanzas of this Ode on Lydia, now apparently in her prime, are in the classical usage of the 'μέν....δέ....' relationship. **Cum tu, Lydia, Telephi ...** contrasts with **Tunc nec mens mihi ...,** as cause and effect. **Telephi cervicem ..., Telephi ... bracchia, meum ... fervens ...iecur, difficile bile ...,** are an avalanche of physical intrusions [Telephus's neck and arm, Horace's liver and bile] that are invoked in Horace by being in the company of Lydia. **Nec mens ..., nec color ..., umor ... labitur, macerer ignibus,** are all the symtoms of distress [hurt feelings, loss of composure, falling tears and burning jealousy] caused by her attention to other men.

Uror ... rixae ... turparunt candidos umeros, 'I burn ... a drunken brawl ... defiles the shining shoulder', is a magnificent summary of drunken revelry and the unease of an older escort, with such a young desirable woman, in such company. **Sive puer furens impressit ... labris,** 'whether a wild youth ... impresses ... lips' compounds the outrage.

Si me satis audias and **non ... speres perpetuum dulcia barbare** 'listen to me - do not expect anything good from such a barbarian' are the immediate and jealous response of a lover in such circumtances. **Laedentem oscula, ... Venus ... imbuit** 'one who would hurt the little mouth that Venus has moistened with nectar' is the reason given implying that he, the lover, suffers from no such lack of reverence and, in consequence, underlying Lydia's lack of excitement about Horace.

Felices ... copula 'three times happier they with secure bonds' must surely compound the lacking quality of Horace the lover, for Lydia. What woman in the midst of the wild party circuit would respond to such words. Her pleasures are immediate, her expectations short term. **Nec malis ... querimoniis divulsus ... suprema ... die** 'nor evil quarrels separate us ... until love is loosened by death' would almost cetainly bring the affair to an end.

This Ode is about Roman society and the party circuit. Telephus is young, handsome and well born; Horace is short and fat, and the son of a freedman with a tendency to social paranoia. Lydia is a healthy and beautiful young woman who responds to flattery and attention, as would be expected. The age old ingredients are there and youth has no respect for convention. Taunting an older man by flirting with his younger partner has always been good as a source of amusement. Everything lies in the response of the older man and Horace allows the situation to get out of hand. This is beautiful poetry wryly set against the poet himself, while commenting on an age old dilemma. Quinn does not see Horace actively involved with Lydia here but acting more in the nature of a confidant, a position surely difficult to substantiate in the first three stanzas; the deep feelings that emanate here are surely motivated by righteous anger at an intrusion rather than those of a disinterested observer. Fraenkel apparently does not consider this Ode worth any attention at all.

ODES I, 25.

Parents of young daughters may well read the first stanza of this Ode with vague feelings of recognition and relief. Young men knocking on shutters at odd hours of the night are symbols of youth, of youth knowing no restraint or acknowledging no conventions. Conversely, the absence of such nocturnal visits is a symbol of growing up, when youth begins to give way to social responsibilities. So, **Parcius ... protervi** and **nec ... adimunt** 'seldom the shaking of shutters and the loss of sleep' need not be taken as the onset of old age but the normal transformation of adolescence into adulthood.

Similarly, **amatque ianua ... cardines** 'the outer door now loves the architrave that once moved on welcoming hinges', need not reflect the constantly opening and closing of a prostitute's front door but the stealthly comings and goings of youthful escapades. This allows us to regard **"me tuo ... Lydia dormis?"** 'the night is young Lydia and you sleep?', free of sinister implications and more in the nature of the hoarse whispers of youthful voices in need of company.

Invicem moechos ... arrogantes flebis 'in turn you will lament the arrogance of lovers' is a sudden switch of emphasis: Horace warns Lydia of what the progression to adulthood holds in store while implying that he has suffered arrogance from Lydia herself. **Anus ... in solo levis angiportu,** 'an old woman alone in a deserted alleyway' is where that progression ultimately leads. It seems reasonable to assume that Horace is using 'old' here to mean to mean no longer attractive, in keeping with the opening stanza, rather than a statement of true age, in order to underline the fact that Lydia has passed the peak of her beauty. It could therefore be regarded as an allegorical warning, a picture of a woman on the streets as the ultimate shame, so beloved of our Victorian ancestors. It is refreshing to find that it was also in use in Roman society. **Thracio ... vento,** 'more bacchante than the Thracian wind under a new moon', is perhaps piling on the agony, picturing the disciple of Dionysus driven to sexual extremes by the hot, dry wind from Thrace and the rampant new moon, lying on its back. **Cum tibi ... equorum ... ulcerosum** 'when burning love and violent desire ... like mares in heat ... wounded by love ... will rage' so Horace completes the picture of Lydia's future degradation.

Non sine questu ... hedera virenti ... pulla ... myrto, 'not without grief that young men prefer greener growths': Horace points out the consequence, that young men prefer younger women. **Aridas frondes ... dedicet Euro,** 'surrendering older branches ... to winter's fires', and, says Horace, consign older, if more experienced, women to more suitable situations.

This Ode on Lydia surprises us. Initially it looks like a counterblast to an old woman who had treated Horace badly; in fact it is presumably prompted by pique and jealousy on Horace's part. Lydia emerges as still a young woman while Horace is telling her that her lifestyle will end in her downfall. Not only does it change our perspective on Lydia but it makes sense of the reconciliation of Horace and Lydia in Ode III, 9. It also prompts the questioning of Lydia's status in Roman society. Hitherto she has been variously regarded as a prostitute, a courtesan or a married woman and adulteress. Here she could be regarded as the daughter of a freedman, a freedwoman on her own part or even part of the Establishment, but, in any case, quite independent as a person.

ODES III, 9.

This Ode is about a Lydia some way removed from the Lydia of the other three Odes. Horace has since had relationships with Glycera and is now involved with Chloe, while Lydia is involved with a younger man, Calais. It is in the form of a dialogue between the old lovers, where one stanza from one partner is followed by one from the other partner and both stanzas follow the same rhythmic formula.

The first two stanzas are remembrances of the old days. **Donec ... tibi,** 'when I was pleasing to you', the scene is set, **nec ... bracchia ... cervici ... dabat** 'nor some better youth was throwing arms around the shining neck'; echoes of Telephus in I, 13? **Persarum ... beatior,** 'I thrived more content than Persia's king,' presumably a standard of lifestyle to which Romans aspired.

This is answered by, **Donec ... Lydia post Chloen** 'when you burned for no other and Lydia was first,' matching Horace's remembrance. **Multi Lydia ... Ilia** 'Lydia flourished in name more so than Roman Ilia', the supreme accolade of Roman womanhood, to be compared with Ilia, mother of Romulus.

The third and fourth stanzas are a statement of their present position with new lovers. For Horace, **me nunc ... Chloe ... citharae sciens** 'Thracian Chloe, skilled in music, rules me now'. Thus his involvement, **pro qua ... mori ... superstiti** 'accordingly I shall not be afraid to die if she is spared', thus his intention.

For Lydia, **me torret ... Calais ... Ornyti** 'Calais burns me with mutual love', thus Lydia's involvement, **pro quo ... mori ... superstiti** 'for whom I will die twice if he be spared', thus her intention.

The fifth and sixth stanzas explore possibilities. **Quid se ... aeneo?** ' 'What if past love returns and gathers us under its yoke?' Horace questions, then elaborates, **si flava ... Chloe reiectaeque ... Lydiae?** 'and golden Chloe is rejected for Lydia?'

Lydia replies, **Quamquam ... pulchrior ... est** 'although he is more beautiful than the stars', and continues disparagingly, **tu levior ... iracundior Hadria** 'and you of no more substance than a cork and angrier than the Adriactic'. She concludes, **tecum vivere ... tecum obeam** 'with you I would live, with you I will die.' Thus, apart from being a delightful work on the subject of reconciliation, this Ode ties the Lydia quartet together and enables us to see Horace and Lydia as believable people; a pair of lovers subjected to the rigours of love's differences. 'Lydia' may well have been pseudonym but was undoubtedly the subject of a real experience in Horace's life.

GLYCERA

INTRODUCTION

The three odes to Glycera form a continuous theme in which Horace is seen to be, in turn, the seducer, the worn out lover and lastly, the jilted lover. In the first two odes he invokes Venus, firstly to lure Glycera into his arms then secondly, to help Glycera see him as a young, vigorous lover. In the third ode, he commiserates with his fellow poet, Tibullus, for being jilted in turn by Glycera while secretly enjoying the spectacle of his rival's misery. All of the odes are magnificently crafted but self mocking to some degree, the first two are quite irreverent while the third has an air of smugness and gloating.

In I, 19 Horace speaks of his love for Glycera and blames Venus for depriving him of his peace of mind and the turmoil that the onset of love has brought. He describes how her beauty has captivated him and of how her impudence has ensnared him. It has caused him to abandon the serious work of writing verse on historical and social commentary. In the final stanza he throws caution to the wind and sets up an altar to his love and asks Venus to bless it with her presence. It is, of course, all a magnificent cover to lure Glycera into a proper frame of mind for seduction.

In Ode I, 30 Horace implores Venus to abandon Cyprus and set up residence in Glycera's 'temple'. Not only that, she should bring Cupid, the Three Graces, the Nymphs, the Goddess of Youth and Mercury as well! A very powerful collection of divinities associated with love and virility. Although Horace pretends this is all for Glycera's sake, it is really on his own behalf that he pleads. He apparently needs all their combined powers to sustain him in his passion for Glycera.

In Ode I, 33 Horace speaks to his friend Albius Tibullus, the poet. Tibullus has been through Glycera's flame also and has been left, jilted. Horace sympathises and although, by implication, he has been jilted also, seeks by example to show that it is happening all the time; he should not write mournful elegies but realise that it is Venus's way. However, it is clear that Horace is paying back his friend for supplanting him in the lady's favour. Horace manages to incorporate several barbed insults within the apparently sympathetic verse.

It would be wrong to take these Odes at face value and impugn them with conventional approaches to the Gods. They are so patently tongue-in-cheek and so cheerfully irreverent. Horace makes himself as much an object of fun as anyone else, taking as his theme, no doubt, the impudence he attributes to Glycera. Yet there are deeply felt references to age and time passing; Horace seemingly has no illusions any more, as to his own amorous abilities, attractiveness or endurance. Despite their innate flippancy there is a pragmatic inner core made very apparent.

ODES I, 19

Mater saeva Cupidinum
Thebanaeque iubet me Semelae puer
Et lasciva Licentia
Finitis animum reddere amoribus.

Urit me Glycerae nitor,
Splendentis Pario marmore purius;
Urit grata protervitas
Et vultus nimium lubricus aspici.

In me tota ruens Venus
Cyprum deseruit, nec patitur Scythas
Et versis animosum equis
Parthum dicere, nec quae nihil attinent.

Hic vivum mihi caesitem, hic
Verbenas, pueri, ponite turaque
Bimi cum patera meri;
Mactata veniet lenior hostia.

GLYCERA 1.

The Cupids' cruel mother,
With the son of Theban Semele, orders me
With wanton licentiousness
To return to loves long since forgotten.

Glycera's elegance burns me,
Shining more purely than white Parian marble;
It burns to behold her beloved face
That so easily slips into excessive impudence.

Venus falling upon me with
A vengeance leaves Cyprus, nor will allow verse
Of Scythians and bold Parthian
Cavalry, nor to say anything not germane to her.

Here for me a live altar, here
Youths, place foliage, incense and two year old
Wine in a libation bowl; a victim
Having been sacrificed, love will come more easily.

ODES I, 30

O Venus, regina Cnidi Paphique,
Sperne dilectam Cypron et vocantis
Ture te multo Glycerae decoram
Transfer in aedem.

Fervidus tecum puer et solutis
Gratiae zonis properentque Nymphae
Et parum comis sine te Iuventas
Mercuriusque.

GLYCERA 2

O Venus, queen of Cnidos and Paphos,
Transfer yourself to the decorous temple
Of Glycera, calling upon you with much incense
Leave beloved Cyprus!

And with you the lambent youth and the Graces
Hurrying with maidenly girdles unloosed, the Nymphs
And, much less obliging without you, the Goddess of
Youth and virile Mercury.

ODES I, 33

Albi, ne doleas plus nimio memor
Immitis Glycerae neu miserabiles
Decantes elegos, cur tibi iunior
Laesa praeniteat fide.

Insignem tenui fronte Lycorida
Cyri torret amor, Cyrus in asperam
Declinat Pholoen; sed prius Apulis
Iungentur capreae lupis,

Quam turpi Pholoe peccet adultero.
Sic visum Veneri. cui placet impares
Formas atque animos sub iuga aenea
Saevo mittere cum ioco.

Ipsum me melior cum peteret Venus,
Grata detinuit compede Myrtale
Libertina, fretis acrior Hadriae
Curvantis Calabros sinus.

GLYCERA 3

*Albius, you must not grieve any more, brooding
In remembrance of harsh Glycera, nor descant
Pitiful elegies why a younger man shines out
And faith has been broken for you.*

*Fair Lycoris with the fabulous profile languishes
With love for Cyrus, Cyrus turns away towards
Frigid Pholoe; but first she-goats will copulate
Together with Apulian wolves,*

*Than Pholoe may transgress with such an ugly lover.
Such the view of Venus who, with cruel brazen jest,
Is pleased to send incompatible hearts and minds
Toward the marriage yoke.*

*As for myself, Myrtal, a freedwoman, more frenzied
And stormier than the Adriatic rounding the cliffs
Of Calabria, has detained me in pleasant bondage
When a better love might call to me.*

ANALYSIS & COMMENTARY

ODES I, 19

This Ode voices, ostensibly, the protestations of a middle-aged Horace against falling in love with a much younger woman. However, its obvious self congratulatory tone fails to convince one of its apparent intent, nor, do we suspect, is it meant to.

Horace begins by claiming that it is all the fault of Venus and Bacchus, **Mater saeva Cupidinum Thebanaeque ... Semelae puer ... finitis animum** 'The inexorable mother of Cupid, in league with the son of Theban Semele, will put an end to the aesthetic life.' The indirect reference to Venus is not intended just as poetical licence but to reinforce the fact that she is notably the mother of cupidity and desire. The indirect reference to Bacchus merely follows on the pattern. The aesthetic lifestyle is most likely a reference to his work as a poet or possibly to a self imposed celibacy. Horace details her orders to him, **iubet et lasciva Licentia finitis animum reddere amoribus** 'and with wanton loves, she is ordering me to restore Licentia.' The import seems clear, Horace is changing his lifestyle, from a poet living as a recluse to the social whirl of dinner parties, drinking to excess and torrid, if short lived, love affairs. We can only assume that Horace may be on the rebound, having taken time to recover from the affair with Lydia.

Horace declares his passion, **urit me Glycerae nitor, splendentis Pario marmore purius** 'The elegance of Glycera burns me, glittering more brightly than Parian marble.' Reinforcing it with, **urit grata protervitas et vultus nimium lubricus aspici** 'the smooth countenance and pleasing impudence burns too intensely to be looked upon.' He comments upon the sudden onset of love and how it is affecting him. **In ... tota ruens Venus Cyprum deseruit,** 'In hastening away, Venus has deserted Cyprus altogether.' **Me ... nec patitur Scythas et versis animosum equis Parthum dicere** 'nor will allow me to tell of Scythian and Parthian cavalry sweeping around, courageous in flight'. **Nec quae nihil attinent,** 'nor of anything, not pertinent to the matter in hand'.

Horace now apparently prepares for the onset of his love for Glycera by preparing an altar for the Goddess Venus with incense, wine and a sacrifice. However, bearing in mind the allegorical nature of the Ode, where sudden love is made the province of Venus and Bacchus, its onset and consequential effect on Horace's work the responsibility of Venus having left Cyprus to torment Horace in person, we should also be prepared to assume that this sacrifice is to be regarded likewise. Since it is all happening out of doors, might it not be in order for us to deduce that he is preparing something in the nature of a barbecue or picnic; certainly something special for his new love! ! **Hic vivum mihi caespitem, hic verbenas, pueri, ponite turaque bimi cum patera meri** 'O slaves, here a living altar, here leafy foliage, place incense and two year old wine with a libation saucer.' One can imagine Horace, in mock solemnity, directing the scene for seduction. When all is complete, the observation, **mactata veniet lenior hostia.** 'When a victim has been sacrificed, she (Venus = love) will come more easily.'

This is a wickedly amusing and cynical Ode, beautifully constructed and contrived with mock solemnity, tongue in cheek, satirising the Roman habit of sacrificing to the Gods on every possible occasion. That it is serious in intent is surely hard to sustain; it is almost certainly of the same genre as Horace's Satires. Horace is here undoubtedly matching the impudence he so much admires in Glycera and writing especially for her. Fraenkel is prepared to accept it as genuine and generally to relegate Glycera to the background, however in a footnote to Ode I, 30, also about Glycera, he comments, 'in Odes i. 19, which is in more than one way related to i. 30, Glycera and Horace's love for her are given their full share' (Fraenkel, <u>Horace</u>, 198, n. 1). Quinn acknowledges that the Ode is born of levity mixed with surprise at being in love again. 'The mockery of conventional forms and attitudes, and the self mockery ... are both evident. The language of the ode is as exaggerated as H.'s reaction ... to the discovery that he still has it in him'. but Quinn still appears to accept the observation of the conventions to some degree, 'a direct appeal to the Goddess, complete with propitiatory offering, ...' (Quinn, <u>Horace The Odes</u>, 161)

ODES I, 30

The apparent intent of this Ode is an invocation to Venus, by Horace, on behalf of Glycera and on the surface appears to be conform to the accepted structure of such a genre. However there are puzzling aspects. Horace begins with a standard approach, **O Venus, regina Cnidi Paphique** 'O Venus, queen of Cnidos and Paphos'. **Sperne dilectam Cypron et ... Glycerae ... transfer in aedem** 'scorn beloved Cyprus and take up residence in the decorous temple of Glycera', **vocantis ture te multo** 'calling upon you with much incense'. An innocent sounding invocation? Glycera is not divinity; why a temple or a shrine? Glycera is, or has been, Horace's mistress so is it to be regarded as a temple of love? In other words how a besotted lover might regard the residence of his mistresses? In which case an invocation to Venus to take residence there, rather than her official residence, is by nature of a romantic hyperbole.

Horace continues to intensify the hyperbole, **tecum ... properentque** 'with you, may they also hasten', fervidus ... puer et solutis Gratiae zonis Nymphae 'the passionate youth, the Three Graces hastening with girdles unloosed and the Nymphs', **Et parum comis sine te Iuventas Mercuriusque** 'and, less obliging without you, the Goddess of Youth and Mercury'. This seems to go well beyond the bounds, even of hyperbole; there must surely be some other motive behind this request for such formidable allies in the battle for love. Horace is plainly in need of help, either to incline Glycera in his favour or, more likely, to reinstate him in her favour. Not only does he need Venus and her helpers but he needs the Goddess of Youth on his side also. Mercury, or Hermes in the Greek, is needed also as the inventor of the Lyre, the God of luck and the God of fertility and presumably, thereby, virility. Horace is apparently in the unenviable position of an older man seeking to satisfy a younger woman and finding it difficult.

Fraenkel has a great deal to say about this Ode, principally because he detects a similarity in form and content to an epigram by Poseidippus, written in the third century BC. However, unlike the original, Fraenkel is not prepared to accept the amorous intent of Horace towards Glycera or her overt, if implied, presence in the work. 'In Horace's ode, on the other hand, Glycera remains completely in the background; it does not matter who she is or what the poet may feel for her. His interest is entirely concentrated on the goddess,' (Fraenkel, Horace, 198). However, Fraenkel agrees that Horace regards the divinities he calls upon in their Greek context but fails to inform us why so many are required and of such diverse talent; Poseidippus was apparently content with just the one. Quinn has doubts about the total validity of the invocation, 'It all still sounds somewhat mysterious' (Quinn, Horace The Odes, 180), but he concentrates upon Glycera as making the plea directly, not Horace doing so on her behalf. There is a subtle distinction here. Certainly Glycera may be the one with a problem, Horace's amorous shortcomings. However, Horace is surely the one that, indirectly perhaps, pleads for help, asking that Glycera, with the help of the divinities called upon, will see him as a more youthful, virile and energetic lover. In short, he is asking Venus and the others to throw over Glycera their magical powers of love that takes away reality and replaces it with an amorous mirage.

ODES I, 33

This Ode commiserates with a friend and fellow poet, Tibullus, over his rejection by Glycera in favour of a younger man, so we must presume that Horace is now over his own infatuation. Whether we can also assume that Tibullus is also the one who supplanted Horace in her affections, must be largely speculative. However, Horace does seem to 'over-egg the cake' rather in his effusive commiserations and there is surely a little smugness in the last stanza!

Horace begins kindly enough, **Albi, ne doleas plus nimio memor immitis Glycerae** 'Albius Tibullus, you must not grieve too much in memory for harsh Glycera.' Horace has changed his view of Glycera obviously. **Neu miserabiles decantes elegos** 'and not descant lamentable elegies,'. It would be best not to put too much emphasis on the word _miserabiles_; from one poet describing the work of another it is altogether too double-edged. Horace explains the reason gleefully, **cur tibi iunior laesa praeniteat fide** 'why for you, faith having been broken, a younger man outshines you'.

Horace now catalogues a list of broken faiths, **insignem tenui fronte Lycorida Cyri torret amor** 'love consumes distinguished Lycoris, with the fine forehead, for Cyrus.' **Cyrus in asperam declinat Pholoen** 'Cyrus turns away towards frigid Pholoe.' **Sed prius Apulis iungentur capreae lupis, quam turpi Pholoe peccet adultero** 'but first she-goats will copulate with Apulian wolves than Pholoe might trangress with so unsightly a paramour.' We note with amusement that the only man mentioned in this catalogue is <u>turpi</u> (foul, unsightly, filthy, at worst - shameful, base, dishonourable at best.) So much for friendship! Also the application of the intellectual knife; as Glycera turned from Horace to Tibullus, so she has turned from Tibullus to another. Never mind, he says, let us blame Venus, **Sic visum Veneri, cui placet impares formas atque animos sub iuga aenea saevo mittere cum ioco** 'so the view of Venus, who is pleased to propel incompatible bodies and minds toward the marriage yoke'. Once again there is a possible double meaning here. Does the incompatibility refer to hopeless love or to eventual consummated love? In other words was Tibullus out of his league? Horace now turns the screw further. He boasts, **Ipsum me melior cum peteret Venus, grata detinuit compede Myrtale libertina, fretis acrior Hadriae curvantis Calabros sinus.** 'As for me, when a better love might call, Myrtale a freedwoman more stormier than the seas of the Adriatic rounding the cliffs of Calabria, detains me in pleasant bondage.'

Fraenkel does not mention this Ode. Quinn is of the opinion that the commiserations on Horace's part are not wholly genuine but attributing Tibullus's grief to the conventions of poetry and that this Ode reveals them <u>ad absurdum</u> as well as containing Horace's own light-hearted view on the matter.

CHLOE

INTRODUCTION

The Odes in this group show Horace's attitude to Chloe some years apart, in years and poetical approach. In the first Ode, he pursues the very young Chloe with clear intentions of seduction. In the second he tries to persuade us that he is finished with love and Chloe can do as she pleases. However Chloe is mentioned in other, intervening poems, so we can assume that she has been more or less a constant factor in his life.

The first Ode is a charming pastoral and Arcadian interlude in which Horace proffers his love with beautiful imagery. If we feel that he is something of an elderly lecher, the language is gentle and soothing. He asks her not to flee like a deer in search of its mother amongst the wild mountains, where she will be even more frightened by the unfamiliar surroundings. He, at least, is not a savage tiger or lion wanting to tear her to bits. She should disentangle herself from her mother's apron strings and start thinking of men.

In the second Ode, Horace uses the imagery of war to liken love to a constant series of battles. He intends to hang up his weapons, which, in the case of love, includes the lyre. He will dedicate it to Venus herself and keep in her temple where he will not be able to use it again. However, to make sure he is not tempted, he intends to lock it away behind barred doors. As a last favour he asks Venus to arouse Chloe in favour of him just once more. Does he wish to test the efficacy of his precautions?

ODES I, 23

Vitas hinnuleo me similis, Chloe,
Quaerenti pavidam montibus aviis
Matrem non sine vano
Aurarum et siluae metu.

Nam seu mobilibus vepris inhorruit
Ad ventos foliis, seu virides rubum
Dimovere lacertae,
Et corde et genibus tremit.

Atqui non ego te tigris ut aspera
Gaetulusve leo frangere persequor:
Tandem desine matrem
Tempestiva sequi viro.

CHLOE 1

Chloe, you avoid me like a new born fawn
Seeking the distraught mother in desolate
Mountains, not without vain
Fear of zephyrs and forest.

For she trembles in heart and limb, whether
The leaves of the briar shiver with the wind or
When the green lizard agitates
The flexible bramble bush.

However, I do not pursue with hostile intent
To tear you apart as the savage tiger or Gaetulean
Lion; pray then, ignore mother,
To seek a man is more appropriate.

ODES III, 26

Vixi duellis nuper idoneus
Et militavi non sine gloria;
Nunc arma defunctumque bello
Barbiton hic paries habebit,

Laevum marinae qui Veneris latus
Custodit. Hic, hic ponite lucida
Funalia et vectes securesque
Oppositis foribus minaces.

O quae beatam diva tenes Cyprum et
Memphin carentem Sithonia nive,
Regina, sublimi flagello
Tange Chloen semel arrogantem.

CHLOE 2

Until lately I served as a soldier, not
Without glory, well suited for love's battles;
Having been discharged from the warfare of love,
The lyre will now reside here. in this temple

Of sea born Venus, whose left side it once
Guarded. Here place a shining white torch, and
Here place the iron bars and steel axes that
Once threatened doors that closed against me.

O you, Divine Queen, who hold blessed Cyprus
And Memphis, absent yourself from Thracian snow,
And with a whip held high in the air
Strike arrogant Chloe one single time.

ANALYSIS & COMMENTARY

ODES I, 23

In this Ode Horace has designs on what seems to be a very young girl and seeks with blandishments to ally her fears at an older man's approach. Initially, he adopts an arcadian approach. **Vitas hinnuleo me similis, Chloe, quaerenti ... matrem non sine ... metu** 'Chloe, you avoid me like a fawn, seeking its distraught mother in desolate mountains, not without needless fears of gentle zephyrs and the forest.' He continues in the same vein, **nam seu mobilibus vepris inhorruit ad ventos foliis, ... et corde et genibus tremit** 'And heart and limb tremble; for whether the leaves of bramble bush trembles with the wind or whether a green lizard agitates the thorn bush'. There is an alternative reading, giving **veris inhorruit adventus** foliis instead of the above: 'the coming of spring trembles the leaves.' There has been some debate on this matter and while the latter version comes well attested, nature purists point out that so early a date would not admit to there being leaves on the bramble, particularly in the high mountains of central Italy. It also might be added that the fawn would be still in the mother's womb, not romping around on its own! Horace then presents himself, **Atqui non ego te tigris ut aspera Gaetulusque leo frangere persequor; tandem desine matrem tempestiva sequi viro** 'However I pursue not with hostile intent to dash you to pieces like a ferocious tiger or Gaetulian lion. Pray then, do not follow your mother, it is more appropriate to seek a man.'

'... we shall hardly be inclined to see in it much more than a pretty little artefact.'(Fraenkel, Horace, 184). Thus Fraenkel dismisses this Ode, having admitted its ornate style and noted its boldness in the Arcadian imagery. Quinn sees it as a study in a young girl's feelings as she reaches puberty and Horace certainly catches the moment very tenderly.

ODES III, 26

In this Ode Horace equates the field of love with the field of war and asks us to believe that he has quitted it for good. Using a military context, he begins, **Vix duellis nuper idoneus et militavi ... nunc arma defunctumque bello ...** 'Up until now I existed well suited for love's battles and I served as a soldier, not without glory; having been discharged from the warfare of love' **Barbiton hic paries habebit, laevum marinae qui Venris latus custodit** 'the lyre, having been carried in battle, will live here, within the temple of sea-born Venus whose left hand side it guards' Horace now defends himself and his lyre against further temptation. **Hic, hic ponite lucida funalia et vectes securesque oppositis foribus minaces** 'Here place a shining white torch and placing here the (metaphorical) iron bars and axes that I used against the doors that love attempted to close against my efforts.' It seems evident that, far from being a reference to axes and levers and weapons of real war, Horace, having placed his lyre in safe keeping, is determined to guard against its further use in the pursuit of love. He directs that it be placed behind locked doors, away from temptation and that all the artifices and aids he used with it, (his poetry?), be laid alongside.

Horace concludes with a mock invocation and plea, **O quae beatam diva ... flagello tange Chloen semel arrogantem** 'O Goddess, you hold well blessed Cyprus and Memphis keeping them free of Thracian snow, O Queen, with a whip held high touch proud Chloe a single time more.' In a malicious finale Horace suggests that Venus arouse Chloe one more time, presumably in his favour, knowing that he can no longer get to his lyre and love will go by default.

Fraenkel does not discuss this Ode and Quinn accepts the military theme of the Ode. However he does assume that Horace is referring to a military engineer, to explain *__vectes securesque ... foribus minaces__*. However the meaning would appear to be metaphorical and entirely in the context of love and its pursuit. Whether we can assume that this late Book III Ode also implies that he intends to write no more poetry at all, as Suetonius implies in his Life, is perhaps too much of a conjectural point.

LYCE

INTRODUCTION

The two Odes on Lyce are separated by some years, physically as well as poetically. In the first, Lyce is seen as a courtesan who can afford to be selective in choosing a lover, keeping Horace at arm's length whenever she chooses. In the second she has become old and no longer attractive, making a pathetic show of herself at parties. In both cases we sense a deeper emotion from Horace than hitherto; in the first he uses scathing language to explain to the lady what she is and what she is about; a businesslike attitude to the service she provides. In the second, he ponders on what has been, what she has meant to him and leads us to believe that she holds a special place in his memory.

Ode III, 10 is a complaint to Lyce that even a Scythian at the extreme edge of barbarity would not treat a lover in such a way. She keeps him out in the rain and snow while she luxuriates in the comfort of her villa. He berates her, saying that she is not in the mould of Penelope, with many troublesome suitors and there is no tapestry she need unwind each night. He almost shouts out the fact that, although she cannot be moved by his plight or by gifts or pleadings, there will be no husband like Odysseus to come and drive him away. He ends by claiming she is a hard woman and no softer than a snake but that if she does not relent soon she need not expect him to wait.

Ode IV, 13 is a reverie that occurs when many years have passed, having seen what has become of Lyce. He cannot gloat too much because the same thing has happened to him: age has overtaken youth. What begins as mocking soon becomes muted as he realises that time is the enemy, not Lyce. In a passionate outburst he remembers Lyce as she was and what she brought to him as an innocent youth. He muses, without cynicism, that time which took Cinara away, has left Lyce to grow into an old crow of a woman. He wonders if the young men, that she now vainly tries to attract, can have any idea of the raving beauty that she once was.

These Odes, together, encapsulate the essence of love and, being so complementary in that respect, are deeply moving. It is impossible to read them without the sense that we all have a common destiny and that all paths lead inevitably to one exit. From the wide perspective that Horace allows us to envisage, we are concentrated, at the last, to a single understanding.

ODES III, 10

Extremum Tanain si biberes, Lyce,
Saevo nupta viro, me tamen asperas
Porrectum ante fores obicere incolis
Plorares Aquilonibus.

Audis, quo strepitu ianua, quo nemus
Inter pulchra satum tecta remugiat
Ventis, et positas ut glaciet nives
Puro numine Iuppiter?

Ingratam Veneri pone superbiam,
Ne currente retro funis eat rota;
Non te Penelopen difficilem procis
Tyrrhenus genuit parens.

O quamvis neque te munera nec preces
Nec tinctus viola pallor amantium
Nec vir Pieria paelice saucius
Curvat, supplicibus tuis

Parcas, nec rigida mollior aesculo
Nec Mauris animum mitior anguibus
Non hoc semper erit liminis aut aquae
Celestis patiens latus.

LYCE I

If you were to live by distant Tanais, Lyce,
The wife of some fierce man, you might lament me,
Extended in desire before your entrance,
Exposed to the Northern elements.

Do you hear how the front door rumbles, and how the
Lovely grove concealed within, echoes, engendered
By the wind, and that the divine will of Jupiter
Glazes the drifted pristine snow.

Place dissenting pride with Venus, no unyielding
Penelope you, with suitors, but born of Etruscan
Parentage. The thread will not go running back
On to the spinning wheel

O you, neither more pliant than inflexible winter
Oak nor, in feeling, more mellow than a Mauretanian
Snake, neither gifts, nor prayers nor the pallor
Of a lover, the colour of a violet

Sways you, yet no wounded husband, detained by love
For a Macedonian mistress, will spare you from your
Suitors. Meanwhile, this body will not always be
Enduring, the theshold or the rain.

ODES IV, 13

Audivere, Lyce, di mea vota, di
Audivere, Lyce: fis anus et tamen
Vis formosa videri
Ludisque et bibis impudens

Et cantu tremulo pota Cupidinem
Lentum sollicitas. Ille virentis et
Doctae psallere Chiae
Pulchris excubat in genis.

Importunus enim transvolat aridas
Quercus, et refugit te, quia luridi
Dentes te, quia rugae
Turpant et capitis nives.

Nec Coae referunt iam tibi purpurae
Nec cari lapides tempora, quae semel
Notis condita fastis
Inclusit volucris dies.

Quo fugit Venus, heu, quove color? Decens
Quo motus? Quid habes illius, illius,
Quae spirabat amores,
Quae me surpuerat mihi,

Felix post Cinaram notaque et artium
Gratarum facies? Sed Cinarae breves
Annos Fata dederunt,
Servatura diu parem

Cornicis vetulae temporibus Lycen,
Possent ut iuvenes visere fervidi
Multo non sine risu
Dilapsam in cineres facem.

LYCE II

The Gods have heard, Lyce, the Gods have heard
My vow, Lyce; you are becoming an old woman yet
You frolic and drink without shame
And wish to seem beautiful and impudent

And, with quivering, drunken song, solicit
Phlegmatic Cupid. He keeps watch over vibrant
Chia with the beautiful cheeks
Said to be skilled in playing the cithara.

For, indifferent, he passes quickly over withered
Oak trees and shrinks from you because of wrinkled
Skin and yellow teeth and
The snowy head that make you seem unsightly.

Neither Coan purple silk nor precious jewels will
Bring back time for you now, which, once it marks
The days belonging to the calendar
Imprisons forever those you may have wanted back.

Alas where has Venus fled with the faultless beauty?
Where the elegance? What have you now of her,
Of her, that once breathed
Love's wonder and took from me my innocence,

Having been known, after Cinara, for perfect beauty?
The fates decreed Cinara a brief span in years, but,
By way of a balance, Lyce,
You were made, by inexorable time,

Into a little old woman the image of an ancient crow
That youth, not without much laughter, might be able
To see only ashes made
From what was once the flame of love.

ANALYSIS & COMMENTARY

ODES III, 10

Horace is once again about the business of seduction and uses contrasted images to gain entrance to the lady's house and her charms. He suggests, **Extremum Tanian si biberes, Lyce, saevo nupto viro** 'If you were living on the banks of extremely distant Tanais, Lyce, the wife to a savagely jealous man'. Having set the supposition, Horace attemps to cash in upon it, **me tamen asperas porrectum ante fores obicere incolis plorares Aquilonibus** 'nevertheless, you might lament with me, extended, before the stormy threshold, exposed to the native north winds.' He embroiders the theme, extending imagination further, **Audis, quo strepitu ianua, quo nemus inter pulchra satum recta remugiat ventis** 'you hear, how with the main gate, the grove of trees, planted within the walls, might echo in the winds.' Then, loading it to extreme, **et positas ut glaciet nives puro numine Iuppiter?** 'and that Jupiter with pristine majesty, glazes the fallen snow?'

Horace now changes his direction and addresses Lyce specifically on her own merits: **Ingratam Veneri pone superbiam, ne currente retro funis eat rota.** 'Place unprofitable pride with Venus, the thread may not go back on to the spinning wheel. And draws a parallel, **non te Penelopen difficilem procis Tyrrhenus genuit parens.** 'No obstinate Penelope you with suitors but born of Etruscan father'. So Horace introduces an Homeric dimension to his entreaties; Lyce should not be like Penelope, undoing her tapestry each night to fool her suitors. Although the meaning of **_ne currente retro funis eat rota;_** can be taken, obliquely, to mean 'lest the tables be turned on you' or 'that all your labours may be in vain' there is undoubtedly a connection to be made with the reference to Penelope and her suitors that follows. The introduction of some mechanical device to explain this passage is really not neccesary; the unwinding of the thread from the tapestry would have involved the rewinding of it back on to its original spool, or spinning wheel, else Penelope's strategy would have been obvious. Horace then renews his plea, describing Lyce unflatteringly,

O quamvis ... te ... nec rigida mollior aesculo nec Mauris animum mitior anguibus 'O you, although neither more pliant than inflexible oak nor, in feeling, more mellow than a Mauretanian snake'. Then he goes on to read the riot act, **neque munera nec preces nec tinctus viola pallor amantium nec vir Pieria paelice sucius curvat, supplicibus tuis.** 'Neither gifts nor prayers nor the pallor of a lover, the colour of a violet, sways you; yet no wounded husband, detained by love for a Macedonian mistress, will spare you from your suitors.' Horace, pursuing the Homeric theme further, with a slighting reference to Odysseus and his love affair with Circe, emphasises that, unlike Penelope, Lyce has no husband to stave off her suitors

In a final couplet, Horace returns to the opening theme, where he is still before the threshold, by now, becoming more plaintive. **non hoc semper erit liminis aut aquae caelestis patiens latus** 'Suffering the heavenly water on the threshold, this side (of his body) will not endure for ever.'

Without wishing to introduce a diverse interpretation, there are puzzling features about the use of ***asperas porrectum ante fores*** in the opening stanza being complimented by ***patiens latus*** in the final stanza. There is a sense that Horace is labouring a point here, not entirely about physical discomfort. Both statements are connected with objects being extended, rigid, full or enduring. We cannot know now what was the Roman euphemism for the male tumescent arousal, but one might assume that Horace, indulging in a play on words, might be constructing a *double-entendre*.on the subject.

Fraenkel does not mention this Ode and Quinn accepts the usual meaning ascribed to the translation of the Ode, especially in lines 8 to 10 and 15 to 16 and 19 to 20. However one is convinced that the Homeric references to the Odyssey hold good and make more sense of what Horace wishes to say. Lyce is not married, she is a courtesan at the very least, but is being difficult and selective about whom she entertains. That Horace knows her well and has visited her many times cannot really be doubted.

ODES IV, 13

On first reading this Ode one might be forgiven for feeling that it has malicious overtones but reflection and re-reading may incline to the opposite view. Lyce is getting old but still clinging on to life and Horace may be casting her as a figure of fun. But then, Horace is old too and feeling it, as may be heard in Odes IV, 1. They are both survivors together and it is not a time for gloating. The content of the Ode is concerned with the thoughts that pass through the poet's mind when he encounters Lyce at a party. The opening stanza should therefore be seen, not as condemnatory, but congratulatory with a triumphant opening. **Audivere, Lyce, di mea vota, di audivere: fis anus** 'The Gods have heard Lyce, they have heard my vow: you are becoming an old woman.' Such a comment, by today's standards, would be uncomplimentary; by the standards of the shorter life expectancy of Horace's day, this need not be so. Then it was a question of survival that was important, not the ageing process. One should be prepared to read the remainder of the stanza in the same context. **Et tamen vis formosa videri ludisque et bibis impudens** 'yet you play and drink and wish to be seen beautiful and impudent'. Horace continues, **et cantu tremulo pota Cupidinem lentum sollicitas** 'and with a tremulous song you solicit phlegmatic Cupid'. Horace draws a gentle comparison, **ille virentis et doctae psallere Chiae pulchris excubat in genis** 'he keeps watch on the beautiful countenance of flourishing Chia, trained to play the cithara.'

Horace nows allows himself to make a personal observation of Lyce and the context is that her age shows and she can no longer expect to attract love. **Importunus enim transvolat aridas quercus, et refugit te** 'indifferent, he avoids you and and flies past the arid oak tree.' **Quia luridi dentes te, quia rugae turpant et capitis nives** 'because yellow teeth, wrinkles in the face and grey hair make you unsightly.' Gently, Horace points out that time is the enemy of all, **nec Coae referunt iam tibi purpurae nec cari lapides tempora** 'neither purple Coan silk nor precious jewels will bring back time for you.' **Quae semel notis condita fastis inclusit volucris dies**, 'which, once it makes the mark establishing the calendar, imprisons forever the days you may have wanted returned.'

Suddenly, as though the previous stanza has let loose the tragedy of the scene within him, Horace shows passion himself. **Quo fugit Venus, heu, quove color? Decens quo motus?** 'Alas, where has Venus fled, or the faultless beauty? Where the elegant deportment?' Horace then reveals his own past involvement: **quid habes illius, illius, quae spirabat amores, quae me surpuerat mihi** 'What have you now of her, of her who once breathed love's wonder and took from me my innocence?' Horace continues the eulogy of use, **felix post Cinaram notaque et artium gratarum facies** 'fortunate and having been known, next in line to Cinara, for perfect beauty and form'. Horace reflects, **sed Cinarae breves annos Fata dederunt** 'but the Fates, although they only allowed Cinara a brief span of years', **servatura diu parem cornicis vetulae temporibus Lycen** 'as a balance they allowed Lyce many days, as though to serve the time of an old crow.' Horace concludes by remembering the past as it was, not as it now might seem. **Possent ut iuvenes visere fervidi multo non sine risu dilapsam in cineres facem** 'so that now, not without much amusement, passionate youth might be able to see only the ashes of decay in what was, once, the very flame of love'.

Fraenkel is deeply moved by this Ode and says so, accepting it for what it is and for what Horace has to say in it. He barely mentions any literary associations with the past but concentrates on the essence of the present. '... none of these earlier poems, ... matches the ode iv. 13 in intensity of feeling and expression, and none contains, embedded in the treatment of a rather repulsive subject, such gems of pure poetry.' (Fraenkel, <u>Horace</u>, 415) Fraenkel waxing lyrical indeed! One can quite forgive him the unfortunate phrase, 'rather repulsive subject', particularly those of us who are growing old ourselves, for such praise. Fraenkel agrees that what seeemingly starts out in ridicule, passes through the stages of pity, passionate grief and regret for lost years, to end on a note of only faint ridicule, 'perhaps to draw a veil over what he has let us see.' (Fraenkel, <u>Horace</u>, 416) Quinn, on the other hand, does not seem to see the passionate self-regret buried in the Ode but merely just another exercise in ridiculing an elderly courtesan who does not know when it is time to stop. He passes over Fraenkel's 'gems of pure poetry' without a great deal of comment and appears to accept the Ode much as the ultimate corollary of the Pyrrha Ode, I,5..

Considering that this Ode is amongst the very last that Horace wrote, when he himself must have been experiencing the same emotions himself, we should accord it as being far more self-revealing than his earlier works. It 'serves in iv. 13 ... as a mirror in which a wider picture can be seen' (Fraenkel, Horace, 415).' It is this wider picture that we must strive to perceive.

LIGURINUS

INTRODUCTION

The two Odes in this section represent a departure in that they are addressed to a specific Roman youth in homosexual terms. Horace is therefore defying strong social taboos without any apparent fear of retribution.

In Ode IV, 1, Horace complains that Venus is urging him to commit himself to love once again despite his age and tries to turn her away towards a younger man, Paulus Maximus, who, he feels, is more suitable for her attentions. There follows what almost amounts to an eulogy of this young man, explaining to Venus the various qualities that make him so suitable. It all seems rather contrived, as though Horace has included a 'bread-and-butter' piece of writing to gain, or retain, favour. We still are left to assume that this is an heterosexual poem particularly since Horace then enters a disclaimer that he is not interested in any of the physical pleasures that life can offer, including the love of youths. Then comes the volte face; Horace precipitates us into his secret passion for Ligurinus. It is still theoretical, only in dreams does he embrace Ligurinus but the imagery is quite vivid and erotic. We are left with the knowledge that that is as far as Horace got in achieving his passion. No social barriers have been breached; dreaming of a young boy's love, by an older man, is not in itself reprehensible.

In Ode IV, 10, it is apparent that nothing physical was achieved or even attempted. Ligurinus is not interested, either in entering into any homosexual relationships with an older man or in such relationships per se. This Ode is therefore a diatribe by Horace in which he points out that the beauty of Ligurinus himself is only transitory, time will change him from youth to manhood and he will lose his present physical attributes very soon. Then, says Horace, he will understand. Simply put, that is the substance of this Ode but many see in it a reflection on old age and lost opportunities. Certainly Horace imbues it with such an underlying feeling; whether this was intentional is uncertain.

ODES IV, I

Intermissa, Venus, diu
Rursus bella moves. Parce, precor, precor.
Non sum qualis eram bonae
Sub regno Cinarae. Desine dulcium

Mater saeve Cupidinum
Circa lustra decem flectere mollibus
Iam durum imperiis: abi,
Quo blandae iuvenum te revocant preces.

Tempestivius in domum
Pauli. purpureis ales oloribus,
Comissabere Maximi,
Si torrere iecur quaeris idoneum.

Namque et nobilis et decens
Et pro sollicitis non tacitus reis
Et centum puer artium
Late signa feret militiae tuae;

Et quandoque potentior
Largi muneribus riserit aemuli,
Albanos prope te lacus
Ponet marmoream sub trabe citrea.

Illic plurima naribus
Duces tura lyraeque et Berecyntiae
Delectabere tibiae
Mixtis carminibus non sine fistula;

Illic bis pueri die
Numen cum teneris virginibus tuum
Laudantes pede candido
In morem Salium ter quatient humum.

LIGURINUS 1

Love! You move once more
To wars long interrupted. I beg mercy, I submit,
I am not as I was under the tyranny
Of wondrous Cinara. Cease, remorseless

Mother of sweet Cupid,
From being ruthless now, to dissuade with gentleness
Ten lustres' stern commands. Go,
Where the entreaties of flattering youth call out.

If you seek a suitable liver
To scorch with passion, to carouse, feasting
On purple winged swans, at the
House of Paulus Maximus, is more appropriate

For he will bear the standard
Of your warfare widely; not silent on clients behalf
A youth of a hundred arts and
Of noble birth, handsome and easily moved.

He will place a marble statue
Under a canopy of citrus wood near the Alban lake
And whatever the abundant gifts
Of rivals, he, more powerful, will laugh.

There, you will inhale
Abundant incense with the nose and will entice the
Mingling of lyre and Berecyntian
Flutes, and not without songs to the shepherds pipe.

There boys with tender maidens
Will be beating the earth twice a day to triple time
Praising your divinity
On dazzling feet in the Salian manner

Me nec femina nec puer
Iam nec spes animi credula mutui
Nec certare iuvat mero
Nec vincire novis tempora floribus.

Sed cur heu, Ligurine, cur
Manat rara meas lacrima per genas?
Cur facunda parum decoro
Inter verba cadit lingua silentio?

Nocturnis ego somniis
Iam captum teneo, iam volucrem sequor
Te per gramina Martii
Campi, te per aquas, dure, volubilis.

*As for me, neither woman nor
Youth benefit me now nor credulous hope of mutual
Sensibility nor contests with unmixed
Wine nor temples encompassed with fresh flowers.*

*But why, alas why, Ligurinus
The occasional tear flows from out of my eyes, why,
With too little eloquence, the tongue
Falls silent in the middle of decorous speech.*

*Now nightly in dreams I pursue
You through the grasses of the Field of Mars,
Through the harshness of the
Inconstant waters. Now, captive, I hold you.*

ODES IV, 10

O crudelis adhuc et Veneris muneribus potens,
Insperata tuae cum veniet pluma superbiae
Et, quae nunc umeris involitant, deciderint comae,
Nunc et qui color est puniceae flore prior rosae
Mutatus, Ligurine, in faciem verterit hispidam:
Dices "Heu," quotiens te speculo videris alterum,
"Quae mens est hodie, cur eadem non puero fuit,
Vel cur his animis incolumes non redeunt genae?"

LIGURINUS 2.

O unfeeling and still powerful with the gifts of Venus,
When unexpected stubble will come upon your pride and
Hair which now floats over the shoulder they will have cut short
And complexion now pink as with the first flower of the rose
Will have turned, Ligurinus, changed into a hairy countenance:
You will say "Alas", how often you have seen another in the
Mirror, "Whose reflection is it today, why was it not the same in
Youth, why do these cheeks not return with character unchanged?

ANALYSIS & COMMENTARY

ODES IV, 1

This Ode has ten stanzas but the middle six stanzas seem to be only loosely connected with the first two and the last two stanzas. Stanzas 1 to 2 and 9 to 10 are about Horace falling in love again at the age of fifty with the youth Ligurinus. Stanzas 3 to 8 are in the nature of a eulogy for Paulus Maximus, a friend of Horace. The connection is not clear at all.

Horace begins by appealing to Venus, **Intermissa, Venus, diu rursus bella moves. Parce, precor, precor. Non sum qualis eram bonae sub regno Cinarae.** 'Venus, you invoke, once more, wars long since interrupted. Have mercy, I beg, I entreat. I am not as I was under the tyranny of wondrous Cinara.' He continues, **desine, dulcium mater saeva Cupidinum, circa lustra decem flectere mollibus iam durum imperiis** 'cease, implacable mother of sweet Cupids, to divert by insiduous commands, almost ten unyielding lustres.' Horace tries to divert her attention, **abi, quo blandae iuvenum te revocant preces** 'Begone! to where the flattering entreaties of youth call to you.' Horace now directs Venus to the house of Paulus Maximus, describing how he is much more in need of her than Horace. **Tempestivius in domum ... si torrere iecur quaris idoneum** 'If you seek a suitable lover to scorch with passion, to feast riotously on purple winged swans, in the house of Paulus Maximus, is more appropriate.' **Namque et nobilis et decens ... late signa feret militae tuae** 'He will bear the standards of your warfare widely ... a youth of a hundred arts ... of noble birth and handsome.'

The paean of praise continues but already suspicions of Paulus Maximus's role in this Ode begin to surface. Knowing already that Horace is sexually attracted to the young man Ligurinus, it must occur to us that Paulus is somewhere involved in the connection. Did they meet at his house? **Et ... riserit aemuli, ... ponet marmoream sub trabe citra** 'He, more powerful, will laugh at the abundant gifts of rivals and will place a marble statue for you near the Alban Lake under a canopy of citrus wood.' **Illic ... duces tura ... delectabere ... carminibus ... fistula** 'There you will receive much incense to inhale and you will take delight in Lyres and Berecyntian flute mingling with songs and with shepherd's pipe.' **Illic bis pueri die ... in morem Salium ter quatient humum** 'There, twice by day, praising your divine command, boys with tender maidens, on dazzling feet, will be beating the ground to triple time, in the Salian manner.' Was Ligurinus one of the youths with dazzling feet?

Horace leaves Paulus Maximus rather abruptly, discounting his own involvement: **me nec femina nec puer ... iuvat ... novis tempora floribus** 'Now, neither woman nor youth nor credulous hope of mutual sensibility nor contests with unmixed wine nor foreheads bound with fresh young flowers gratifies me now.' Horace then addresses the youth, Ligurinus. **Sed cur heu, Ligurine, cur manat rara meas lacrima per genas? ... cadit lingua silentio?** 'Why, then, Ligurinus, why flows the unaccustomed tear from the eyes? Why the eloquent tongue falls silent, with too little decorum, in the middle of speech?' Horace admits to his passion for Ligurinus: **nocturnis ego somniis iam captum teneo, ... sequor ... te per aquas, dure, volubilis.** 'Nightly, in dreams, now I hold you, now, winged, I pursue you across the grass of the Field of Mars, now, hard to the touch, through swirling water.'

Fraenkel feels that this Ode is by way of being an overture to the whole of Book IV and, as such, contains a little of all the elements to be encountered therein; love, the praise of famous people, the problems of growing old and the resignation it entails. As an explanation of the apparently unconnected elements within this Ode, it is certainly one point of view. If it were not Horace under consideration one might be tempted to regard the middle stanzas as so much literary padding: well crafted but not within the expected context. Quinn is rather dismissive, seeing the Ode mainly as a vehicle for the praise of Paulus Maximus, of whom he quotes a disparaging Epigram by Cassius Severus. 'You are almost eloquent, you are almost beautiful, you are almost rich; just one thing you are not almost; good for nothing!' So much for the <u>centum puer artium</u> of Horace.

It is with an apparent air of diffidence that Horace introduces Ligurinus in the last two stanzas and if we are to accept that this is the predominant idea behind the Ode, then the almost surreptitious nature of his inclusion is puzzling. It has been pointed out by several writers that Ligurinus is a

Roman name and that by making his homosexual emotions for the youth known, Horace was flouting convention in a marked way. Even at the age of fifty and with a successful reputation to support him, it would seem foolish. One could suppose that within the social circle in which Paulus Maximus moved the affection was acceptable but we cannot know.

BOOK IV ODE 10

This is a rather sad little Ode constructed as one long sentence divided into a metrical structure of eight lines. It is sad in many ways; Horace contemplating the indifference of Ligurinus to his pleas, Ligurinus contemplating, if unknowingly, the end of childhood, ourselves, the readers, marking the passage of time for both Horace and the youth and also the inexorable pre-knowledge that for Horace, at least, only a few years remained.

Initially, Horace addresses the youth, **O crudelis adhuc et Veneris muneribus potens** 'O unfeeling [youth] hitherto powerful with the gifts of Venus'. Warning him of what will happen, **insperata tuae cum veniet pluma superbiae** 'when unexpected stubble will come upon your pride'. **et, quae nunc umeris involitant, deciderint comae** 'and, of the hair which now floats over the shoulder, they will have cut off', **nunc et qui color est puniceae flore prior rosae mutatus, Ligurine, in faciem verterit hispidam** 'and the complexion, which now is pink, as with the flower of the first rose, changed, Ligurinus, and will have turned into a hairy countenance'.

Horace now places the narrative into the mouth of Ligurinus. **Dices "heu," quotiens te speculo videris alterum, "quae mens est hodie, cur eadem non puero fuit, vel cur his animis incolumes non redeunt genae?"** '"Alas," you will say then, for the many times you have seen another you in the mirror, "whose reflected presence is it today, why not the same youth as it was, or why cannot these cheeks return to their former glory, without damage to the ego?."'

Fraenkel says of this Ode, 'The real theme of Horace's poem is not, as it may first seem, disappointment in the pursuit of παιδικὸς ἔρως, but something more simple and touching, regret for the bygone days of youth.' (Fraenkel, Horace, 414) He cites, as support for this, Petrarch's epistle, 'De brevitate vitae' which uses a quotation from this Ode. Fraenkel concludes that it is Horace who really speaks through Ligurinus, voicing his own regret. Quinn tends to agree: 'the opposition is not between youth's missed opportunities and the denial of love's pleasures which old age brings, but between Ligurinus as he is now ... and as he soon will be ...' (Quinn, Horace The Odes, 317/8). There is a difference of emphasis between Fraenkel and Quinn but the positions that they adopt are not unreconcilable.

The more simplistic view is, of course, that this Ode merely updates the situation with which we are left at the end of Ode IV, 1. Horace, having expressed homosexual desires to the youth, has been rebuffed and in a fit of pique tells him that his beauty will not last. Adolescence and manhood will overtake his youthful beauty and he will have nothing with which to attract further attention. Yet we have no clear indication that Ligurinus is interested in homosexual approaches; the fact that he attracts them is no proof of reciprocity on his part. Unless we assume that he belongs to the intimate circle of Paulus Maximus where he would be expected to observe whatever rules were tolerated. The theme of regret for lost youth that emanates strongly from this Ode may just be accidental; it can certainly stand on its own as a lecture from a disappointed suitor.

ADVICE TO OTHERS

INTRODUCTION

The four Odes in this group are all fairly lighthearted in character, amusing and semi-serious at the same time. Horace remains objective throughout and advises, impartially. In II, 4, he advises a friend that falling in love with a slave girl is nothing to be ashamed of; such famous figures as Achilles and Ajax had fallen in love with captive women. Even Agamemnon, while besieging Troy, had taken time off for dalliance. Becoming practical, Horace adds, you never know your luck, she may be the daughter of a king and, in any case, so lovely and faithful is she that she cannot be of common stock. He hastens to add that, although he praises her beauty, there is no need for jealousy, he is far too old to be interested in her himself.

In II, 5, he speaks to another friend, advising him not to be too precipitate in attempting to make love to a young girl, emphasising that she is far too young for his lustful intentions. She is still of an age to play with her friends, not to enter into cohabitive domesticity. He cautions that unripe fruit is best left to mature on the vine, nature will eventually run its course and although patience will add years to him it will bring fulfilment to her. Then she will seek a lover of her own accord becoming more beautiful and desirable than either a certain Pholoe or Chloris. More beautiful even than Cnidian Gyges. Patience is the word!

II, 8 is different again. This time Horace addresses the lady concerned directly, a well known flirt and utterly faithless. He castigates her for her shameless infidelity and her worthless oaths. He charges that she renders love worthless by her behaviour, that there is no constancy any more and that even the Gods of love laugh outright at her protestations. He points out that every youth growing into manhood will eventually come under her spell, and that they will then join in the increasing number of her slaves from whom none are willing to depart. He sympathises with the wives and parents of the men she holds captive by her charms.

In III, 15, Horace addresses a certain Chloris, the wife of humble Ibycus, who had been famous for her beauty but now, quite elderly, has not the sense to withdraw from the party scene. He points out, a little cruelly, that she is nearer to her funeral than the glories of her youth and that cavorting amongst maidens is making her ridiculous. He suggests that she pass on to her daughter her experience and be content to live the life of a respectable Roman matron and concentrate on knitting!

These are delightful Odes but not strong in dramatic content, nor were they intended as such. They are amusing examples of social comment of the time but are really timeless in their implication. One could put contemporary names to the individuals described therein, if not from one's own experience then from a casual exploration of today's more lurid media coverage. Then, as now, the advice was valid; now, as then, one knows it would be unheeded. One should not complain, however, were one certain that it would, once again, produce such magnificent poetry.

ODES II, 4

Ne sit ancillae tibi amor pudori,
Xanthia Phoceu. Prius insolentem
Serva Briseis niveo colore
Movit Achillem;

Movit Aiacem Telamone natum
Forma captivae dominum Tecmessae;
Arsit Atrides medio in triumpho
Virgine rapta,

Barbarae postquam cecidere turmae
Thessalo victore et ademptus Hector
Tradidit fessis leviora tolli
Pergama Grais.

Nescias an te generum beati
Phyllidis flavae decorent parentes:
Regium certe genus, et penates
Maeret iniquos.

Crede non illam tibi de scelesta
Plebe dilectam neque sic fidelem,
Sic lucro aversam potuisse nasci
Matre pudenda.

Bracchia et voltum teretesque suras
Integer laudo; fuge suspicari,
Cuius octavum trepidavit aetas
Claudere lustrum.

PHYLLIS

*Love for a maidservant should not be shameful
To you, Phocian Xanthias. Formerly the slave girl
Briseis, with snowy complexion, moved
Proud Achilles.*

*The beauty of captive Tecmessa moved her master
Ajax, son of Telamon; Agamemnon blazed with fire
For a captured maiden in the
Middle of triumph,*

*Allowing the victor of Thessaly to cut to pieces the
Barbarian host and, Hector having fallen, delivered
Pergamos over to the exhausted Greeks,
To be more easily destroyed.*

*You cannot know whether, as son-in-law, the parents
Of golden Phyllis, surely of regal descent, will
Honour you with riches and she must mourn
Cruel household Gods.*

*Believe that one so faithful, so beloved to you, so
Disinclined to avarice, is not from the common herd
Nor could be born from a mother of whom
She ought to be ashamed.*

*I praise countenance, arms and graceful calves quite
Free from desire, put to flight suspicion of one
Whose lifetime, with eight lustrums passed,
Hastens to its close.*

ODES II, 5

Nondum subacta ferre iugum valet
Cervice, nondum munia comparis
Aequare nec tauri ruentis
In venerem tolerare pondus.

Circa virentes est animus tuae
Campos iuvencae, nunc fluviis gravem
Solantis aestum, nunc in udo
Ludere cum vitulis salicto

Praegestientis. Tolle cupidinem
Immitis uvae: iam tibi lividos
Distinguet autumnus racemos
Purpureo varius colore.

Iam te sequetur (currit enim ferox
Aetas, et illi, quos tibi dempserit,
Apponet annos), iam proterva
Fronte petet Lalage maritum,

Dilecta, quantum non Pholoe fugax,
Non Chloris, albo sic umero nitens,
Ut pura nocturno renidet
Luna mari Cnidiusve Gyges,

Quem si puellarum insereres choro,
Mire sagacis falleret hospites
Discrimen obscurum solutis
Crinibus ambiguoque vultu.

LALAGE

*She is not yet strong enough to bear the yoke
Upon the neck, nor yet be equal to the duties
Of a consort or be forced to tolerate
The roughness of a bull in sexual frenzy.*

*The spirit of your young woman is about the fields
Now assuaging the oppressive heat of the sun in
Flowing water, now desiring much more
To play with other young things within moist*

*Willow plantations. Rise above the desire for
Unripe fruit; already the stalk has a bluish tint
For you and soon Autumn will adorn
Completely with a manifold purple colour.*

*Soon she will follow you (for time runs on unbridled
And it adds to her stature, the years it disposes
From you), soon with impudent forwardness,
Lalage will reach out for a lover,*

*To be esteemed more highly, not as transient Pholoe
Nor Chloris, with shoulder so shining white as when
The alabaster moon shimmers over the
Nocturnal sea, and Cnidian Gyges,*

*Who, if intermingled with a crowd of maidens, might
Deceive the stranger, even with extraordinary senses
The dividing line having been obscured
With loosened hair and ambiguous countenance.*

ODES II, 8

Ulla si iuris tibi peierati
Poena, Barine, nocuisset umquam,
Dente si nigro fieres vel uno
Turpior ungui,

Crederem. Sed tu simul obligasti
Perfidum votis caput, enitescis
Pulchrior multo iuvenumque prodis
Publica cura.

Expedit matris cineres opertos
Fallere et toto taciturna noctis
Signa cum caelo gelidaque divos
Morte carentes.

Ridet hoc, inquam, Venus ipsa; rident
Simplices Nymphae ferus et Cupido,
Semper ardentis acuens sagittas
Cote cruenta.

Adde quod pubes tibi crescit omnis,
Servitus crescit nova, nec priores
Impiae tectum dominae relinquunt,
Saepe minati.

Te suis matres metuunt iuvencis,
Te senes parci miseraeque, nuper
Virgines, nuptae, tua ne retardet
Aura maritos.

BARINE

*If any penalty for forsworn vows
Had ever done harm to you, Barine,
If you might be made more ugly by one
Blackened tooth or nail,*

*I might believe. But no sooner have you bound
Your faithless word with vows than you gleam more
Beautiful, much younger and become a universal
Object of desire.*

*It is expedient to swear falsely upon the ashes
Of a mother, the secrets of Apollo, the silent
Icy cold constellations of the entire night sky
And the deathless Gods.*

*I say this, it ridicules Venus herself; they laugh
Out loud, the uncomplicated Nymphs and the unruly
Cupid, always sharpening his glowing arrows upon
A bloodstained whetstone.*

*The adult male population always increases, new
Ones served by you also increases nor previous ones
Abandon the roof of the reprobate mistress
But threaten often.*

*For the young men's sake, their mothers go in terror
Of you, old men to be spared unhappiness with you,
Brides, but recently virgins, lest your radiance
Detain their husbands.*

ODES III, 15

Uxor pauperis Ibyci,
Tandem nequitiae fige modum tuae
Famosisque laboribus;
Maturo propior desine funeri

Inter ludere virgines
Et stellis nebulam spargere candidis.
Non, si quid Pholoen, satis
Et te, Chloris, decet: filia rectius

Expugnat iuvenum domos,
Pulso Thyias uti concita tympano.
Illam cogit amor Nothi
Lascivae similem ludere capreae;

Te lanae prope nobilem
Tonsae Luceriam, non citharae decent
Nec flos purpureus rosae
Nec poti vetulam faece tenus cadi.

CHLORIS

Consort of wretched Ibycus,
Set a limit to your wantonness and renowned
Activities now, at last;
When nearly ripe for a funeral, cease

To play among maidens
And to scatter a miasma upon the shining stars.
If what becomes Pholoe
Suits you not enough; more suited your daughter

To storm young men's houses,
Beating the drum that summoned the Bacchanale.
She compels Nothus's love
In the manner of a frolicsome nanny-goat;

Old woman, neither the lyre
Nor the rose's purple blossom, nor drinking as far as
The dregs from a wine jar, becomes you,
The famous Lucerian shorn wool, next to you, does.

ANALYSIS & COMMENTARY

ODES II, 4

Horace addresses Xanthias, his friend, who has fallen in love with a slave girl and quotes several examples from mythology by way of reassurance. He goes on to say that being a slave girl there is no knowing her antecedents; Xanthias might be on to a good thing. He finishes by stating that his passion is on behalf of his friend; he has no interest in the girl himself!

Horace begins, **Ne sit ancillae tibi amor pudori, Xanthia Phoceu** 'Love of a maidservant should not mean a feeling of shame for you, Phocian Xanthias.' Continuing with examples, **prius insolentem ... movit Achillem, movit Aiacem ... captivae dominum Tecmessae; arsit Atrides ... virgine rapta, ... et ademptus Hector ... tolli Pergama Grais** 'Formerly Briseis moved proud Achilles ... captive Tecmessa ... moved Ajax ... Agamemnon blazed for a captive maiden ... while successfully besieging Pergamos.' Thus in the first twelve lines Horace reassures his friend that there are many illustrious precedents, before descending to the mundane. **Nescias ... te ... Phyllidis flavae decorent parentes**, You cannot know whether the parents of golden Phyllis are rich and will honour a son-in-law.' **Regium certe genus, et penates maeret iniquos** 'maybe of royal descent, and how she must lament such cruel household Gods'. Horace offers further reassurance, **crede non illam ... plebe ... sic fidelem, sic lucro aversam ... matre pudenda** 'believe that one so faithful, ... so averse to gain is not of common stock ... not born of a shameful mother.'

Horace excuses his passionate outburst, **bracchia et vultum ... laudo; fuge suspicari cuius ... trepidavit aetas claudere ...** 'I praise her ... but please do not be suspicious ... my life hastens to its close!'

Fraenkel does not admit this Ode to his commentary at all. Quinn sees it as an amusing interlude, a view with which it is difficult to quarrel. It says more about Roman family life and values than it does about love and the semi-serious suggestion that Xanthias might end up marrying a servant-girl is very tongue-in-cheek. At the same time it gives an insight into just who was likely to become slaves of the Romans whose net of conquest was very wide. Horace's own disclaimer of an erotic interest in Phyllis is not

- 148 -

too be taken too seriously; at forty Horace would have still been in full flight as regards amorous intent. This is an Ode best enjoyed for its own sake alone.

ODES II, 5

This Ode cautions restraint, on the part of a friend, in rushing his fences in the pursuit of what seems to be a young girl. The gist is that patience is required until the girl reaches the age of awareness, when she is likely to make the first move herself.

Horace begins by restraining his friend from behaving like a bull in frenzy, **Nondum subacta ferre iugum valet cervice, ... nec tauri ruentis ... tolerare ...** 'She is not yet strong enough to bear the yoke upon the neck, ... nor to tolerate the roughness of a bull in sexual frenzy.' He explains that she is still at the age of a child and of playing games with friends, **circa virentes est animus tuae campos iuvencae, ... in udo ludere cum vitulis salicto praegestientis** 'The spirit of your young woman is still about the fields, ... desiring to play with young friends in willow plantations.' He advocates patience, **tolle cupidinem immitis uvae: ... distinguet autumnus racemos purpureo varius colore** 'Rise above lust for unripe fruit: ... autumn will soon adorn with manifold purple.' Eventually will come the reward, **iam te sequetur ... iam proterva fronte pete Lalage maritum** 'Soon she will follow you ... soon, eager for knowledge, Lalage will seek a lover.' **Dilecta, ... non Pholoe ... non Chloris ... Cnidiusque Gyges** 'beloved, ... as was not Pholoe, ... nor Chloris ... and even Cnidian Gyges. Horace concludes, **quem si puellarum insereres choro, ... sagacis falleret hospites ... solutis crinibus ambiguoque vultu** 'who, if placed within a group of maidens, ... might deceive even a stranger with keen senses ... with loosened hair and ambiguous countenance.'

Fraenkel does not include this Ode in his book on Horace and Quinn regards it as a counterpart to Ode I, 5. There an experienced woman, an inexperenced man; here the reverse although the point here is also that age is also a significant differential. Quinn makes the assumption that the two are already married and that Lalage is a child bride of thirteen or so. This fact does not seem to be implied. Even though the man is not named, Lalage is surely too significant a name for there to be any doubt on identities. Socially, even in the easygoing circles inhabited by Horace and his friends, the subject of such a sensitive marriage would hardly be made the subject of such light hearted poetry. One must accept that the liaison is somewhat less formal than that, most probably a master/slave relationship, upon which public comment would be acceptable.

ODES II, 8

This Ode is more a censure than advice; Horace berates Barine for the easy way in which she will swear affection with no intention of observing it. The suggestion has been made that Barine is not a real person but a type and Horace is speaking for all men in his castigation of such behaviour. He begins directly, **Ulla si iuris tibi peierati poena, Barine, ... dente si nigro ... una turpior ungui, crederem** 'If any penalty for faithlessness ever caught up with you, Barine, ... a blackened tooth ... an ugly nail, I might trust you.' Then, enumerating her faults, **... sed tu simul obligast perfidum votis ... prodis publica cura** 'But no sooner have you sworn your faithless vow ... you become an object of universal desire.' **Expedit matris cineres ... fallere ... divus morte carentes** 'To swear falsely by the ashes of a mother ... by Apollo ... by the stars and by the deathles Gods, is expedient.' Horace, indignant, explains how her behaviour denigrates the meaning of love, **Ridet hoc, inquam Venus ipsa; rident ... Nymphae ferus et Cupido** 'I say this, it ridicules love itself; ... making Cupid and the Nymphs laugh out aloud ...' Horace comments on the demoralising effect she is having on his contemporaries, **adde quod pubes tibi crescit omnis, servitus crescit nova, nec priores ... relinquunt ...** 'Added to which the adult male population grows up to serve you, adding to that already serving you, while the elderly do not abandon you, although they often threaten to do so.' Horace concludes, by commenting acidly on the feelings of their wives and parents, when she places them in such jeopardy: **te suis matres metuunt ... te senes parci miseraeque, nuper virgines, nuptae ... retardet aura maritos** 'Mothers and elders ... fear your beauty will detain their sons or newly wedded brides, their husbands.'

Fraenkel has no reference to this Ode and Quinn sees it as 'a lightheated attack (however ostensibly indignant) upon that notorious liar Barine, ('the girl from Bari') ... a variation upon ... the theme that lovers are not punished by the Gods ... if they break their promise of undying love: ...' (Quinn, Horace The Odes, 212). One cannot quarrel with that sort of diagnosis, it is certainly in the vein of semi-serious exasperation mixed with a little admiration. One does wonder, however, whether Horace was personally involved and was one of the growing population of admirers. It is certainly an interesting observation of Roman mores.

ODES III, 15

This Ode is addressed, if not out loud, to a woman who, although still bent on having a good time, is getting on in years and is making a fool of herself. She is married and since both she and her husband are named we can assume that, psuedonyms or not, she is a matter of common gossip. Horace begins forcibly and to the point, **Uxor pauperis Ibyci, tandem nequitiae fige modum tuae famosisque laboribus** 'Wife of poor Ibycus, set a limit now, at last, to your wantonness and renowned activities.' **Maturo propior desine funeri inter ludere virgines et stellis nebulam spargere candidis** 'Of ripe age and nearer to a funeral, cease to play amongst maidens and to scatter a cloud upon the shining stars.' Horace addresses. in his mind, the lady herself: **non, si quid Pholoen, satis et te, Chlori. decet** 'What is suitable for Pholoe, Chloris, is not fitting for you' He suggests that her daughter is more of an age for such behaviour: **filia rectius expugnat iuvenum domos, ... illam cogit amor Nothi ... ludere capreae** 'more fitting the daughter takes by storm the houses of young men ... love of Nothus compels her to play like a frolicsome roe deer.' In mock despair, Horace utters a final admonition, **te lanae prope nobilem tonsae Luceriam, non citharae, nec ... rosae nec poti vetulam ...** 'old woman, neither the lyre, nor the rose, not the dregs of a draught of wine become you; better the wool of Luceria to wear around you'.

Fraenkel ignores this Ode, as properly too lightweight to draw a satisfactory literary comparison. Quinn suggests the Ode is advice to an ageing courtesan that it is time to hand over to her daughter and accepts, as such, that it was not intended to have any dramatic context at all. Certainly this Ode cannot compare with Ode III, 10, to Lyce, as regards dramatic context. Which may serve to underline how different is Horace's intensity of feeling when he is personally involved with the woman in question than when he is, as in this case, merely an observer. Yet one cannot observe and distinguish the nature of these two Odes and continue to maintain that Horace was not a lover himself; the objective nature of this Ode compared with the anguish of his Odes to both Lyce and Lydia bears witness to this.

FRIENDSHIP

INTRODUCTION

The two Odes within this group have been isolated from the many devoted to friends because one senses that more than mere friendship is implied and that deeper emotions, reciprocated or not, motivated Horace.

Ode II, 12, far from being the simple poem that many commentators assume it to be, can be seen to have a far deeper meaning. It is addressed, ostensibly, to Horace's patron, Maecenas, and concerns the poet's reluctance to write epic poetry on the theme of Caesar Augustus and his military exploits. African Numantia is mentioned specifically but the general feeling is that the poet is rejecting military vainglory wherever it might happen. Horace suggests that it is more properly the subject of narrative prose, not epic verse, and that Horace is not the man for either the subject matter or the manner in which it should be portrayed. At their most simplistic level, the meaning of the first three stanzas is simply a statement of fact, but what follows leads us to question this. Is Horace making a profound statement of moral, if not artistic, values? That the grim realities of existence are matters for factual statement rather than creative literature and that self-aggrandisement is no excuse for forcing art into uncompromising moulds?

In the next three stanzas Horace demonstrates, by means of a bewitching profile of Maecenas's wife, Terentia, the difference in values between art used properly and art completely bastardized. It is a pointed dig at Maecenas that his mind concentrates on false verities while the real values in his life lie unseen beneath his eyes. Horace finishes with a last stanza that has the ephemeral quality of envy for another's good fortune and, seemingly, an unstated passion for another man's wife. Encased in a tender, rather personal, observation of affection between a man and wife, lies a yawning abyss of emotion that obviously was never explored.

In the second Ode, Horace evokes awakening Spring as the beginning of the remorseless cycle of Nature which, compared to mankind's brief years, is endless. He passes on to man's occupation with approaching death as an end to all consciousness, of how time is so precious and its retention so impossible. He counsels that in our passage through life we should make the most of all things; what we leave becomes the province of our heirs. At the last he mentions the name Torquatus and one realises that this is a question of farewell, from one friend to another, and that all that has gone before in this Ode has been leading to this one moment. What has seemed to be an emotionless, objective appraisal of the grim facts of existence now become intensely poignant. Horace ends with a comparison to the classical myths, emphasising that the physical aspects of death and farewell are not the most important factor; it is that one friend proceeds into a veil where remembrance is no more, while the other is left with memories intact.

ODES II, 12

Nolis longa ferae bella Numantiae
Nec durum Hannibalem nec Siculum mare
Poeno purpureum sanguine mollibus
Aptari citharae modis,

Nec saevos Lapithas et nimium mero
Hylaeum domitosque Herculea manu
Telluris iuvenes, unde periculum
Fulgens contremuit domus

Saturni veteris: tuque pedestribus
Dices historiis proelia Caesaris,
Maecenas, melius ductaque per vias
Regum colla minacium.

Me dulcis dominae Musa Licymniae
Cantus, me voluit dicere lucidum
Fulgentis oculos et bene mutuis
Fidum pectus amoribus;

Quam nec ferre pedem dedecuit choris
Nec certare ioco nec dare bracchia
Ludentem nitidis virginibus sacro
Dianae celebris die.

Num tu quae tenuit dives Achaemenes
Aut pinguis Phrygiae Mygdonias opes
Permutare velis crine Licymnae,
Plenas aut Arabum domos,

Cum flagantia detorquet ad oscula
Cervicem, aut facili saevitia negat,
Quae poscente magis gaudeat eripi,
Interdum rapere occupat?

TERENTIA (LICYMNIA)

*You may not wish the long wars of wild Numantia,
Nor unforgiving Hannibal, nor the Sicilian Sea
Purple with Carthaginian blood, to be adapted to
To the gentle measure of the lyre,*

*Nor Hylaeus and the Lapithae savage with too much
Unmixed wine and the taming, by Hercules, of the
Sons of the Earth, from which perilous situation
The glittering of ancient Saturn*

*Trembled violently: You will be better at telling
Narratives of the past Maecenas and, in simple prose,
Of Caesar's battles and hostile Kings having been led
By the neck along the highways.*

*For me the Muse is the sweet singing of Mistress
Licymnia, it has willed me to speak of brightly
Flashing eyes and honourably constant heart
Overflowing with mutual love,*

*To lift a foot with dancing girls loses her no grace
Nor to contest a joke nor to extend an arm in salute
To the glittering maidens, taking part on the day
Of renowned Diana's sacred rites.*

*You may not wish to exchange the hair of Licymnia's
Head for all that wealth which Archaemenes held
Or the Mygdonian riches of fertile Phrygia
Or the plenitude of Arabian homes,*

*As she bends aside the nape of the neck towards eager
Kisses or with mock severity deny them since she may
Rejoice more to have them stolen by him who embraces
Sometimes demanding to steal herself.*

ODES IV, 7

Diffugere nives, redeunt iam gramina campis
Arboribusque comae;
Mutat terra vices et decrescentia ripas
Flumina praetereunt;

Gratia cum Nymphis geminisque sororibusque audet
Ducere nuda choros.
Immortalia ne speres, monet annus et almum
Quae rapit hora diem.

Frigora mitescunt zephyris, ver proterit aestas
Interitura, simul
Pomifer autumnus fruges effuderit, et mox
Bruma recurrit iners.

Damna tamen celeres reparant caelestia lunae;
Nos ubi decidimus,
Quo pius Aeneas, quo Tullus dives et Ancus,
Pulvis et umbra sumus.

Quis scit an adiciant hodiernae crastina summae
Tempora di superi?
Cuncta manus avidas fugient heredis, amico
Quae dederis animo.

Cum semel occideris et de te splendida Minos
Fecerit arbitria,
Non, Torquate, genus, non te facundia, non te
Restituet pietas;

Infernis neque enim tenebris Diana pudicum
Liberat Hippolytum,
Nec Lethaea valet Theseus abrumpere caro
Vincula Pirithoo.

TORQUATUS

Already the foliage returns to the trees and the herbage
To the fields to disperse the snow;
The earth mutates the interchange and the decreasing rivers
Pass by between their banks;

The Grace with twin sisters and the Nymphs venture forth
To lead the dance unclothed.
The year and hour, which carries off the indulgent day, advises
You not to hope for immortality.

Winter's colds grow mild, the West Wind supplants Spring, about
To be lost to Summer, likewise
Fruit bearing Autumn pours forth its harvest and by and by
Hastens back inactive Winter.

Nevertheless, the swiftly changing moons repair the damage; but
We, when we have fallen to lie
Where virtuous Aeneas, whither rich Tullus and Ancus, are only
Dust and insubstantial shadow.

Who knows whether the Gods of the upper world may add tomorrow's
Time to the sum of today?
Everything which you dedicate to your friendly spirit will escape
The eager hand of the heir.

When once you have perished and Minos has made his illustrious
Judgement concerning you,
Torquatus, neither family nor eloquence from you, nor sense
Of duty will reinstate you;

For Diana may not release virtuous Hippolytus from the deathly
Darkness of the lower regions
Neither has Theseus strength enough to tear away the Lethean
Bonds of precious Pirithous.

ANALYSIS & COMMENTARY

ODES II, 12

This Ode is usually regarded as a *recusatio* in which Horace evades a request from Augustus, not to mention pressure from Maecenas, to write an epic Ode on the military glories of Rome under Augustus. He does this by concentrating on the grace of Maecenas's wife, Terentia, whom he calls Licymnia. 'The Ode is both artificial and overladen', Fraenkel suggests and, further, 'the poem as a whole will probably leave most readers cold ...' (Fraenkel, Horace , 219). Not, one ventures to suggest, if it is regarded with lateral thought. Having successfully labelled and categorized it with its Grecian origins, Fraenkel is happy to regard all reference to Licymnia as an appendage to the *recusatio*. Whatever the motives of Horace in writing this Ode, it undoubtedly conceals a *de facto* moral statement against the vainglories of war and the artificial values that man and society place upon them. To attribute to it the mere contrivance of a *recusatio* is to diminish not only the stature of the Ode itself but that of Horace also.

Horace commences with exactly that theme, **Nolis longa ferae bella Numantiae nec durum Hannibalem ... purpureum sanguine mollibus aptari citharae modis** 'You would not wish the sweet measures of the lyre to be adapted to the long standing wars of wild Numantia, nor unforgiving Hannibal or the Sicilian Sea purple with Carthaginian blood'. He continues the parable with reference to the mythical past, **nec saevos Lapithas mero Hylaeum domitosque Herculea ... contremit domus Saturni veteris** 'neither indeed, Hylaeus and the Lapiths, savage with too much unmixed wine, nor the taming, by Hercules' hand, of the sons of the Earth, whence the house of Saturn trembled violently'. Horace suggests, tongue in cheek, that Maecenas and his style of writing are better suited to the theme of war, **tuque pedestribus dices historiis proelia Caesaris ... vias regum colla minacium** 'better if you tell in prose, narratives of Caesar's battles, Maecenas, and the menacing kings led by their necks along the streets.'

The implication of these opening three stanzas is quite clear: war is a matter of history and politics, the proper subject of prose narrative. It is not the proper function of creative art to recreate sordid fact and glorify the darker side of man's nature. Neither is its function to eulogise the victor of a conflict. There is never a real victor; mankind itself is the only real loser.

Horace now concentrates on what should be the real issues for Maecenas, his good fortune in his home life. It is here that we may detect envy in Horace and undertones of passion for Terentia; passion that he could not address openly. Thus the <u>recusatio</u> becomes double-edged; under its shadow Horace is able to pour out his own feelings for another man's wife. **Me dulcis dominae Musa Licymniae cantus, ... mutuis fidum pectus amoribus** 'for me, the sweet singing of Mistress Licymnia, me, the Muse willed to speak of brightly flashing eyes and constant heart overflowing with mutual love.' Having tuned into the theme of Licymnia's gracefulness, Horace continues, **quam nec ferre pedem dedecuit choris ... virginibus sacro Dianae celebris die** 'for her to lift a foot with dancing girls loses her no grace, nor to contest a joke nor extend an arm to the glittering maidens that celebrate Diana's sacred day.' Horace addresses Maecenas directly, **num tu quae tenuit dives Achaemenes ... permutare velis crine Licymniae, ... aut Arabum domos.** 'You would not wish to exchange a hair of Licymnia for that which rich Achaemenes held or the Mygdonian wealth of fertile Phrygia or the overflowing plenty of Arabian houses.' In the final stanza Horace appears to indulge in what might seem to be a masochistic reflection of Maecenas's good fortune and his own envy. **Cum flagrantia detorquet ad oscula cervicem ... interdum rapere occupet?** 'When she turns away to allow eager kisses on the neck, or with mock severity, deny them, since she may rejoice to have them stolen from him who demands more, sometimes she may anticipate and snatch a kiss herself.'

This Ode is surely something more than a throwaway gesture by a poet unable, or unwilling, to carry out a commission. To damn it with faint praises, '... rich in delicate touches', '... a side issue of, a wholly heterogeneous theme', and similar (Fraenkel, <u>Horace</u>, 219), is to do it a massive injustice. The theme is quite homogeneous; a perfect whole in which Horace questions moral values, expresses distaste for the superficial gestures aimed at self-aggrandisement and concentrates the essence of the Ode into his own secret yearnings that cannot hope for fulfilment. Quinn observes 'his warmly passionate, elegantly-phrased depiction of himself ... as the poet in love ...'. Quinn further notes, 'Horace ironically deprecates his chosen form, though he can hardly have failed to hope that Maecenas would appreciate the new, serious use ...'. (Quinn, Horace The Odes, 220).

ODES IV, 7

This Ode, apparently pastoral in context, links the seasons of the year with man's own immortality; the ultimate irony being that Nature recovers, man does not. However, buried deep within this Ode, is a personal note. A certain Torquatus is addressed as though he will shortly be subject to this inevitable process and in the final stanza Horace laments with him that like Pirithous, friend of Theseus, once descended into Hades, Torquatus will drink from the River Lethe and forget Horace. This has the effect of turning this Ode from a pastoral elegy into a deeply felt poem of farewell. As such it is a testimonial to a close friendship. Whatever the context one might wish to attribute to such a friendship is immaterial; the Ode stands as a magnificent memorial to Torquatus.

Horace begins, imperceptibly, **Diffugere nives, redeunt iam gramina campis arboribusque comae; ... flumina praetereunt.** 'Already the foliage returns ... to disperse the snow.' **Gratia Nymphis ... ducere nuda choros. immortalia ... monet ... rapit hora diem** 'the Grace with Nymphs ... lead the dance naked. The year and the hour ... advises ... not to hope for immortality.' **Frigora mitescunt zephyris, ver proterit aestas ... pomifer autumnus ... bruma recurrit iners** 'Winter's cold gives way ... Summer replaces Spring ... fruitful Autumn bears forth ... inactive Winter returns.' Horace having pictured the inexorable cycle of nature, enters a comparative note on the human cycle: **damna tamen celeres reparant caelestia lunae: nos ubi decidimus ... pulvis et umbra sumus** 'The swiftly changing moons repair the damage ... but we, when we have fallen ... are but dust and shadows.' Emphasising the random nature of survival, **Quis scit an adiciant hodiernae crastina summae tempora di superi? ... amico quae dederis animo** 'Who knows whether the Gods of the upper world will add tomorrow to the sum of today? Everything thing that you dedicate to your own loving self shall escape the avaricious hands of your heir.'

In the last two stanzas, Horace relates all that has already gone before to what seems to have been an intense, personal relationship and the Ode reaches its climax of farewell. **Cum semel occideris et de te splendida Minos fecerit arbitria, non, Torquate, genus, non te facunda, non te restituet pietas** 'When once you have perished and Minos has pronounced his royal verdict concerning you, Torquatus, neither family, nor eloquence, nor sense of duty will reinstate you.' Horace ends with classical allusions, where Diana tries to bring Hippolytus back to life after his chariot fall and Theseus, descended into the underworld, fails to awaken Pirithous from his eternal sleep. **Infernis neque enim tenebris Diana pudicum liberat Hippolytum, nec Lethaea valet Theseus abrumpere caro vincula Pirithoo** 'for neither can Diana release virtuous Hippolytus from the unending darkness of the lower regions, nor has Theseus the strength to break the Lethean bonds of beloved Pirithous.'

Fraenkel insists on linking this Ode with the earlier Ode, I, 4 and while the two have a common theme, the earlier clearly lacks the intense motivation of the latter and certainly lacks the polish and the understated, but doubly powerful, imagery that accompanies it. Fraenkel, no doubt, is more comfortable if he can find a literary comparison but one finds it to be very strained in this instance. However, once freed from his compulsion to find literary parallels, Fraenkel has some very fine things to say about this Ode but tends to relegate Torquatus to the role of a 'let us now praise worthy men' insertion. He does not seem to regard him as being of any personal concern of Horace beyond a footnote and, alas, another comparison, 'The affectionate last two lines recall the end of iii. 4' (Fraenkel - Horace, 420 Note 3). Quinn also draws comparison with Ode I, 4, but is quick to point out the essential differences rather than the superficial similarities. He does, however, pick up the importance of the allusion of Theseus and Pirithous to Horace and Torquatus, '... Pirithous chained by the River of Forgetfulness; ... has forgotten his friend; Theseus still remembers' (Quinn, Horace the Odes, 313).

STRANGE ENCOUNTERS

INTRODUCTION

The two Epodes in this section are clinical descriptions of individual encounters between the younger Horace and an elderly woman. Whether it is the same woman in both instances is not clear but in both the narrative appears to be of Horace's private thoughts.

In the first Epode, Horace, stung by a taunt of impotence, catalogues the appearance of the woman in objective, clinical terms and points out that he cannot be expected to rise to the occasion when faced with such physical deficiencies. Although the surroundings are luxurious and the atmosphere intellectual, he requires a great deal of stimulus before he can complete the task. Superficially it is a wry, amusing work but there are undercurrents which lead one to enquire why Horace finds it necessary to be there in the first place.

In the second Epode, Horace has been hurriedly summoned to the lady's house and is a little incensed by the peremptory nature of the summons. He has received gifts from the lady and is therefore beholden to her but plaintively enquires why the hurry. But the lady is impetuous and leaves him no time for recriminations and when, as might be expected, his body fails to respond she vilifies him for being immature, inconsistent and finding her unattractive. Horace closes the Epode without comment.

These two Epodes are usually avoided because of their explicit content but, on examination, there is no real obscenity. The sexual act is dealt with in a matter-of-fact manner, the description of the lady's cosmetic endeavours are quite amusing, if chauvinistic and the joke is really against Horace himself. There is no overt maliciousness; the narrative is more in the nature of a raconteur telling stories against himself.

These two works date from Horace's early years, years presumably when he was short of money and searching for patronage. There is certainly no perception of love in them and even lust is made noticeable by its absence, at least on the part of Horace. It has been suggested that they were mere exercises in invective *iambi* after the style of Archilochus but their common theme and the intensity with which Horace pursues it is puzzling. Having read them, one can hardly escape the feeling that Horace is speaking from experience, so detailed is the observation of an older woman's physiological attributes. As to her extravagant sexual appetite, Horace makes it entirely believable. If one is prepared to accept that these were born of experience, then the love poetry of Horace is rendered all the more believeable and his matter of fact approach to the subject more understandable. Presumably, if one has plumbed the depths anything that follows must be in the nature of an anticlimax. One can be objective but still appreciative.

EPODE 8

Rogare longo putidam te saeculo,
Vires quid enervet meas,
Cum sit tibi dens ater et rugis vetus
Frontem senectus exaret,

Hietque turpis inter aridas natis
Podex velut crudae bovis!
Sed incitat me pectus et mammae putres,
Equina quales ubera,

Venterque mollis et femur tumentibus
Exile suris additum.
Esto beata, funus atque imagines
Ducant triumphales tuum.

Nec sit marita, quae rotundioribus
Onusta bacis ambulet.
Quid quod libelli Stoici inter Sericos
Iacere pulvillos amant?

Inlitterati num minus nervi rigent,
Minusve languet fascinum?
Quod ut superbo provoces ab inguine
Ore adlaborandum est tibi.

1.

To imply that my virility is losing strength, you, so foul
With sustained debauchery;
With a blackened tooth and a forehead that decrepit age has
Ploughed across with wrinkles;

Between withered buttocks, hairless private parts gape with
All the shamelessness of a cow!
A bosom with the kind of flapping breasts that belong more
To fecund mares, a soft undulating

Belly and swollen calves added on the end of slender thighs;
Really fills me with desire!
Be happy, and indeed may your many triumphs lead your funeral
Procession with their images.

May no offended wife equipped with well rounded berries
Happen to be passing by.
Why therefore do they love to throw pamphlets of Stoic
Philosophy amongst silken cushions?

Do illiterate sinews stiffen any more or the phallus languish
Any less for all of that?
Therefore it is up to you to bring about arrogance from below,
You must incite it with the mouth.

EPODE 12

Quid tibi vis, mulier nigris dignissima barris?
Munera cur mihi quidve tabellas
Mittis, nec firmo iuveni neque naris obesae?
Namque sagacis unus odoror,
Polypus an gravis hirsutis cubet hircus in alis,
Quam canis acer, ubi lateat sus.
Qui sudor vietis et quam malus undique membris
Crescit odor, cum pene soluto
Indomitam properat rabiem sedare, neque illi
Iam manet umida creta colorque
Stercore fucatus crocodili, iamque subando
Tenta cubilia tectaque rumpit.
Vel mea cum saevis agitat fastidia verbis:
"Inachia langues minus ac me;
Inachiam ter nocte potes, mihi semper ad unum
Mollis opus. Pereat male, quae te
Lesbia quaerenti taurum monstravit inertem,
Cum mihi Cous adesset Amyntas,
Cuius in indomito constantior inguine nervos,
Quam nova collibus arbor inhaeret.
Muricibus Tyriis iteratae vellera lanae
Cui properabantur? Tibi nempe,
Ne foret aequales inter conviva, magis quem
Diligeret mulier sua quam te.
O ego non felix, quam tu fugis, ut pavet acres
Agna lupos capreaeque leones!"

2.

Why the violence woman, most suitable from black elephants?
For what reason send letters to me with gifts
I am not a muscle bound youth nor one of delicate nose?
Yet with a fine sense of smell alone I detect,
As does a sharp dog the pig lying concealed, you nourish the
Goat like a polyp resides in an hairy armpit.
As she hastens to assuage untamed passion from a penis quite
Unready, what a strange smell arises from all over
The skinny body arising more than anything from the artificial
Complexion of crocodile droppings and Cretan chalk
That stays moist. Now by taking the action upon herself, the bed
Covering splits asunder, being strained too far.
And also she ridicules my fastidiousness with savage words:
"With Inachia you languish much less than with me:
You drain Inachia three times a night, for me the action is always
Soft at once. May she perish painfully, that
Lesbia who, when trying to find a bull, recommended slothful you,
When Amyntas of Cos might have wasted himself away
For me, within whose indomitable pubic zone is placed a mighty
Sinew more constant than a young mountain tree.
For whom do they hurriedly spin, for a second time, the new shorn
Wool with the purple dye of Tyre? For you
To be sure, for it would be amongst the company of her equals that
The woman could choose no better than you.
Oh, unhappy me, that you take flight, as the lamb fears severity
From wolves and the roebuck from lions."

ANALYSIS & COMMENTARY

These two Epodes are not really about love at all, but lust. Lust, not emanating from Horace but for Horace from much older women and it is made implicit that their lust is, *per se*, for any man; Horace is merely the unfortunate man of the moment. One may well ask, why? These are works of Horace's earlier years, years, presumably, when he was still reinstating himself into Roman society after his return from Philippi. We know that he was penniless and we must also assume that he was glad of any help, whatever its source. If acting the part of a gigolo was the price of survival, and ultimate public esteem, he would not have been alone in that predicament. That is, of course, attributing personal motivation to these two Epodes but another school of thought would have them as exercises in invective iambi, copying Greek models such as Archilochus or Hipponax. Certainly this theory would fit well with enthusiastic, youthful expeditions into obscenity under the guise of art but, even so, one senses that there is, in both examples, an undercurrent of personal involvement; as though the clear, unpleasant pictures evoked are the result of actual experience rather than fertile imagination.

EPODE VIII

It must be assumed here that Horace, intent on carrying out his part of an abhorrent physical encounter, carries out an inner conversation with himself. Only by adopting a jocular approach to the matter in hand can he hope to remain intellectually detached from his actions. He commences, in an unspoken answer to his partner's charge of lack of interest. **Rogare longo putidam te saeculo, vires quid enervet meas.** 'To imply that my virility is losing strength, by you [of all people], rotten with sustained debauchery'. Horace now catalogues his partner's defects, not in a vindictive way but more in the nature of a boost to his own, presumably, intact. **Cum sit tibi dens ater ... vetus frontem ... exaret, hietque turpis inter aridas natis podex velut crudae bovis!** These are meant to be detached, objective observations of an elderly woman's physical attributes. One should not invest them with unecessary obscenity; they are precisely what a younger man would note in his elderly partner. Neither should they be disregarded since they are an integral part of the poem.

'With a black tooth, a forehead that decrepit old age has ploughed with wrinkles, hairless private parts, that gape between withered buttocks, with the same crudity of a cow.' Horace attempts to introduce levity, **sed incitat me pectus et mammae putres, ... venterque mollis ... exile suris additum.** 'But it is the bosom with flapping breasts, the kind belonging to fruitful mares, the soft belly and thin thighs with swollen calves added on, that really fills me with desire.'

Horace continues in a cynical vein, supposing that the lady's lovers would have a short life, **esto beata, funus atque imagines ducant triumphales tuum** 'Be happy! Indeed, may your triumphs lead the funeral with their images.' **Nec sit marita, quae rotundioribus onusta bacis ambulet** 'May no offended wife, with well rounded berries [presumably berry-shaped breasts], pass by.' The translation of *rotundioribus bacis* is obviously an euphemism for well-shaped breasts and is obviously meant as a contrast to his current partner The comparison intended is unclear unless a counter-attraction is suggested. Horace contemplates the luxurious surroundings and questions whether the company of wealth is really worth all of this and whether it is sufficient to help him complete the task. **Quid quod libelli Stoici inter Sericos facere pulvillos amant?** Questioning whether stiff Stoic literature may stiffen his resolve, and other things; whether making love on soft silken pillows helps matters at all. 'Why therefore do they like to throw pamphlets of Stoic philosophy between Chinese silken pillows?'

Horace concludes that they do not, **inlitterati num minus nervi rigent, minusve languet fascinum?** 'Do illiterate sinews stiffen any more or the phallus languish any less?'

Horace completes the Ode by admitting that, whatever else, he will need his partner's help in completing the task. **Quod ut superbo provoces ab inguine ore adlaborandum est tibi.** 'Therefore, it is for you to bring about arrogance from the privy member, you must incite it by manipulating with the mouth.' So, with a plaintive cry for help, Horace concludes. We should accept this last couplet in the general context of the whole work and of today's liberated view of sexual encounters, where oral stimulation is taken very much for granted. Fraenkel finds it polished but repulsive, blaming it on the Greeks and on Horace's friend, Catullus.

EPODE XII

Horace again in the company of an elderly woman and again indulging in a conversation to himself as he tries to act the lover. This time. it would seem, the lady has sent her maid to demand his presence, having already showered him with gifts and letters. Horace is offended by the peremptory nature of his summons. **Quid tibi vis, mulier nigris dignissima barris?** 'Why the rush, woman, which is more suitable to black eleohants?', Horace enquires. We can only assume that _nigris barris_, refers to the military war elephants, used at the charge, and is the Roman equivalent to our 'bull in a china shop'. Horace seeks an explanation for this sudden action: he is not particularly young nor does he belong to the nobility, the 'delicate noses', **munera cur mihi quidve tabellas mittis, nec firmo iuveni neque naris obesae?** 'Why send presents to me with letters, I am not possessed by youth nor of a delicate nose?' Horace levels an accusation, **namque sagacius unus odoror, polypus an gravis hirsutis cubet hircus in alis, quam canis acer, ubi lateat sus** 'And yet, with a fine sense of smell alone, I have an inkling you nourish the old goat as an unwholesome polyp may reside in a hairy armpit, as much as does a keen smelling dog, where a hog may lie concealed.', thus suggesting that the lady retains her libido and her many gifts now have to be paid for.

Qui sudor vietis ... undique membris crescit odor, cum pene soluto ... rabiem sedare 'As she hastens to allay untamed passion from a penis that is unready, what perspiration and what an unpleasant odour arises from the withered limbs, and that Cretan chalk complexion tinted with crocodile droppings is now becoming moist and already, by taking the action upon herself, the bed covering, having been stretched to its limits, bursts.' So Horace, having been summoned, is taken unawares by the lady's passion.

Seeing his unwillingness and his loathing, his partner turns on him with exasperation, **vel mea cum saevis agitat fastidia verbis** 'And also she ridicules my fastidiousness with savage words.' Horace now gives a voice to his partner. **"Inachia langues minus ac me; Inachiam ter nocte potes, mihi semper ad unum mollis opus."** '"With Inachia you weary much less than me; you avail Inachia three times a night, for me you soften the working part at once."' She curses Lesbia (presumably the friend) who seems to have recommended Horace to her. **"Pereat male, quae te Lesbia quaerenti taurum monstravit inertem, cum mihi Cous adesset Amyntas, cuius in indomito constantior inguine nervos, quam nova collibus arbor inhaeret"** "'May she die unpleasntly, Lesbia who, seeking a bull, discovered slothful you, when Amyntas of Cos might have wasted himself away for me, in whose invincible pubic zone is stuck a sinew more constant than a young mountain tree.'" His partner comments sneeringly upon his social standing, **muricibus Tyriis iteratae vellera lanae cui properabantur?** "'For whom hurry they to spin again the new shorn wool with purple dye of Tyre?'" **Tibi nempe, ne foret aequales inter conviva, magis quem diligeret mulier sua quam te.** "'For you to be sure, for would it not have been among the company of her equals, that the woman would choose better than you.'" She finishes with a lament, **"O ego non felix, quam tu fugis, ut pavet acres agna lupos capreaeque leones"** "'O I am unhappy, that you take flight, as lambs fear wolves and roebuck, lions.'".

Fraenkel comments that this Epode, in relation to the woman, is more fully worked out than Epode VIII, and that the lamentations of the elderly woman owe something to Hellenistic erotic poetry, but still finds the subject matter repulsive. One cannot really agree. Plain spoken certainly but on examination, it is a quite believable statement of an encounter between a young man, in need of of patronage, and an elderly, rich woman prepared to help, at a price. The narrative is objective and, taken in that context, not overly obscene or intended as such. If poetry is life encapsulated in a metrical structure, then all is grist to the mill; that Horace should extend his vision is in no way at fault and certainly not to be ignored.

ENVOI

POSTSCRIPT TO THE LIFE OF HORACE

Fraenkel's major work on Horace leaves us with the clear, magnificent image of the professional poet but with only the vague, two-dimensional image of the man himself, one with whom it is virtually impossible to come to terms as a person of human virtues and failings. Quinn's more pragmatic work on the Odes allows us to see a little way behind the profile of the perfect poet, enough for us to want to know much more about this creative genius than the substance of his poetical output. But both of these authors seem content to leave Horace's poetic methodology to speak for the man as well as the poet, as though that were sufficient in itself. With diffidence, it is suggested that this cannot provide the total answer nor unlock the enigma of the man himself. Without wishing to enter into any Existential philosophical argument, creative genius is a natural force that is shaped by environment, upbringing and experience. It is only the output of such creative genius that may be initially constrained and directed by external conventions. The maturing of that creative genius, to bring out any measure of innovation, must proceed by way of experience itself rather than by copying what has gone before.

To seek out the real man behind the inscrutable face that history has assigned to Horace it has been necessary to look, not at his epic and laudatory poetry but at his personal poetry. For it is only by searching for inter-personal relationships that one is able to observe the private, as opposed to the public face of the man himself. The poetry of real, emotional love is the one genre in which there is little striking of false attitudes or of self posturing in such personal relationships. The deep emotions and all the rigours of love expose the true character of a man. By assuming the love poems to be autobiographical and the record of a set of sequential events in his life, it has been possible to gain a glimpse of human side of Horace. It is hoped that in creating a sort of inner life of Horace, this book has served to flesh out the bare bones of Suetonius's Life of Horace and equip them with the frailities and strengths of the common man and help form the persona of a living, breathing individual

When Horace returned to Rome, after Philippi, he would have been in his early twenties, the age of the angry young man. Whether he had begun to write love poetry by that time cannot be verified but examination of his output would certainly place Epodes 8 and 12 and Satire 1, 2. within that period. Horace is certainly the indignant, angry young man in these two Epodes and very much the arrogant, self-certain and uncompromising youth in the Satire. Epode 8 is not just about the lusts of older women but it contains a young man's contempt for the rich life and the intellectual pretensions that are often part of it. Hence the silken cushions and the Stoic pamphlets; the harsh descriptions of the idle rich and the way they seek and demand their pleasures. Epode 12 is also a youthful diatribe; against the power of wealth and how it can command any service it chooses by the exercise of that power, the imtemperance it allows its possessor, the artifices it attracts and the utter lack of moral scruples to which it descends. The woman buys Horace with money and gifts and treats him as merchandise that must provide pleasure. Satire 1, 2. is a young man's view of sexual gratificaton for its own sake, one in which any notion of love is absent. In an older man what would appear as world weary cynicism emerges as a succession of simplistic, youthful vignettes in stark black and white; there is never a hint of a compromising grey. It can in no way be seen to be chauvinistic, only as a youthful, superficial comprehension of an enjoyable activity shorn of any deeper relationship.

In Epode 12 Horace is seen to be already involved with Inachia but in Epode 11 he is at least three years older and recovering from his first serious bout of being in love. Inachia has passed out of his life, presumably to another man, and Horace has realised, belatedly, that there is much more to love than mere sexual gratification. There is still a residue of the angry young man where Horace flaunts convention and the advice of friends by seeking a homosexual relationship with Lyciscus thereby showing scorn for further heterosexual affairs. However, Epode 15 shows Horace involved, heterosexually, with Neaera, having presumably parted with Lyciscus after a very short time. He is unlucky again, Neaera is involved with another man, one who can offer her riches with which Horace cannot compete. Horace is bitter and vestiges of the angry young man are still visible. In Epode 14, he has the friendship and influence of Maecenas to help but possibly resents his dependence upon it since he is very ascerbic in reply to an assumed criticism. Once again he is having trouble in his affairs with women, this time with a freedwoman named Phryne. He neatly turns the criticism back on Maecenas by reminding him of his own dependence on the young actor Bathyllus. However, by the time he wrote Ode I, 5 Horace is clearly over his angry young man stage. In this Ode to Pyrrha there is a touching maturity and acceptance that love often takes far more than it gives; that the rewards it offers are like harvests and must be reaped and enjoyed as they occur. There is no guarantee that they will perpetuate.

Lydia is a major factor in Horace's life for during her dominance he grows from angry young man to maturity. In the first of four Odes, I, 8, he is an observer of her power over men, particularly his friend Sybaris, who is swept off his feet by the emotion of the moment, forgetting his friends and his masculine pursuits. In Ode I, 13 he becomes involved himself and finds himself the possessive lover, jealously guarding his beloved from his friends and behaving foolishly himself. Already we see that Horace has passed beyond youth sufficiently to see them, not as rivals, but possessing the attributes of youth with which he now cannot compete. In Ode I, 25, Horace is the passed-over lover once again but anger is now replaced by a philosophic acceptance. Rather than castigate Lydia for choosing another he reminds her that time is on his side rather than hers and that, in turn, she will suffer the same indifference. Ode III, 9, is an effervescent work, bubbling over with joy, sly humour and a sense of the ridiculousness that love, in retrospect, confers upon its participants. It is by a mature Horace, in years and poetical craftmanship, written much later in his life and after being involved with Glycera and Chloe.

Horace's affairs with Glycera and Chloe are the real watershed in his life because we sense that, during this time, Horace reaches the years of discretion where he begins to question whether the pursuit of love as a pleasure is really worth the effort it requires, both mentally and physically. Glycera is really too hot for him to handle and the very young Chloe, although a sop to his middle-aged vanity, is the quintessimal adolescent still partially imprisoned in childhood. More and more Horace has to call on divine help. In Ode I, 19, he addresses Venus, blaming her for filling him with desire for the young Glycera and saying that he is now mature and past such frivolous, young love. Yet he admits that he is flattered by the attentions of this younger woman and is prepared to behave accordingly and play the youth again. We see him, now rich and established, with the help of servants, setting the scene for her seduction. But, in Ode I, 30, he again appeals to Venus to bring with her, Juvena the Goddess of Youth and Mercury, the God, among other things, of virility. The implication seems obvious. There is a feeling of relief in Ode I, 33, when he commiserates with a friend at having been jilted by Glycera and admits that he, now rid of Glycera himself, is passing time with the freedwoman, Myrtal. The two odes to Chloe end this phase in his life when he admits that he has reached a stage where he intends to pursue love no more. Ode I, 23, records his attempt to attract the love of a very young girl, still at her mother's side. Ode III, 26, records his disillusion with the whole business of love, vowing to lay down his arms in the warfare of love. He invokes Venus one more time to awaken Chloe to his desires but his heart is not really involved.

With Lyce Horace enters full maturity where the pursuit of love is at a more gentle pace and where mutual satisfaction is the aim of both parties. In Ode II, 10, he addresses Lyce in matter-of-fact terms pointing out the realities of their respective situations and advising her against striking false attitudes when their mutual need is self evident. In Ode IV, 13, some years have passed when he meets Lyce again and while admonishing her for failing to give age its due is struck with the sudden realisation that it has overtaken them both. Ligurinus is a Roman youth and the subject of two late odes in which Horace is attracted by his youthful beauty. No longer the angry young men with a desire to shock, it is by no means clear if Horace's interest is physical but since the love does not appear to have been consumnated, except in Horace's dreams, it is perhaps not relevant to even speculate. Certainly these are the last of the recognisable love poems, Horace is fifty years of age, successful, assured in an easy lifestyle and women are no longer a challenge. The youth Ligurinus must have represented as much a vision of lost youth as an object of desire and with him the wheel seems to have turned full circle.

The poems written specifically for friends, such as Lycimnia and Torquatus, those containing advice on problems of love, such as Phyllis and Lalage and the critical poems to Barine and Chloris, do not add substantially to what may be obtained from the poems where he himself is actively involved in close relationships. The life that can be construed from a study of the love poems is cohesive and believable. Horace is seen to progress through recognisable stages as a living human being rather than a professional poet. He experiences grief and joy, he comments rationally on life in general and is seen to be as fallible as the rest of us in matters of the heart. It allows us to renew our love of his poetry with the knowledge that it was written not only with the precision of perfect and immaculate poetical vision but with the common fears and frailities of the ordinary man.